RENAISSANCE
HANDWRITING

Also by Alfred Fairbank

★

A HANDWRITING MANUAL

RENAISSANCE HANDWRITING

An Anthology of Italic Scripts

by

Alfred Fairbank

and

Berthold Wolpe

THE WORLD PUBLISHING COMPANY

Cleveland and New York

Published by The World Publishing Company *2231 West 110th Street, Cleveland 2, Ohio*

Library of Congress Catalog Card Number: 60–11133

FIRST EDITION

ACKNOWLEDGEMENTS

THE authors wish to express their gratitude for permission to reproduce scripts accorded to us by:

The British Museum; the Public Record Office; the Victoria & Albert Museum; the Soane Museum; the Bodleian Library, Oxford; St. John's College, Cambridge; the Fitzwilliam Museum, Cambridge; the Vatican Library; Laurenziana, Florence; Zentral Bibliothek, Zurich; the Cambridge University Press; the Oxford University Press; Mr. and Mrs. Philip Hofer; Mrs. Priscilla Gill; Signor Giovanni Mardersteig; Mr. Paul Standard; and Miss Anna Hornby.

By the courtesy of Mr. J. H. Pafford, we were allowed the use of the Library of London University, which has a fine Palaeographical Department.

Researches made by Alfred Fairbank were facilitated by the grant of a Leverhulme Research Award and he takes this appropriate opportunity to express publicly his thanks. He is also grateful to Mr. H. R. Hughes and Miss Anna Hornby for translations from Italian made by them.

Berthold Wolpe wishes to record his appreciation of help received from friends at Faber's, especially from Mrs. E. M. Hatt, and from Miss Albinia de la Mare.

The text indicates clearly the debt owing to Dr. Stanley Morison and the late James Wardrop for their articles on italic scripts.

Thanks are due to Mr. R. G. Hawkins and Fine Art Engravers for the care they took in making the blocks.

CONTENTS

NOTE

THE woodcuts in the text are taken from the following books printed at Venice:

Half-title; Francesco Colonna's *Hypnerotomachia Poliphili*, 1499.

Title-page, p. 15, p. 49; Sigismundo Fanti's *Theorica et pratica de modo scribendi*, 1514.

P. 47; G. A. Tagliente's *Lo presente libro insegna*, 1524.

PLATES

INTRODUCTION
by Alfred Fairbank

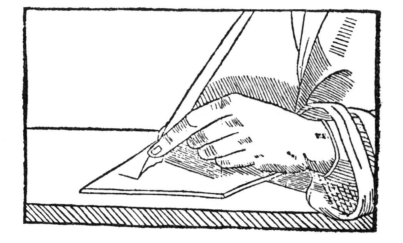

INTRODUCTION

FOR longer than a thousand years there has been a continuous if varying interest in handwriting as an artistic craft. Those who were concerned that manuscripts should be of fine quality may have been patrons as important as kings and popes, courts and the Church, or penmen, such as professional scribes with ideals of craftsmanship, or writing-masters, skilful and proud, depending upon their clever impressive performances to gain a public and pupils. And, of course, for centuries there has been the interest of numberless non-professional penmen, who in writing letters, journals, and notes, were doing something they regarded as worthwhile and were minded to do it well. Naturally the need to read easily what is written has retained high standards in the exercise of writing.

The position today is that we are emerging from a general and degrading view that the typewriter, which gives a quick service to legibility, has therefore robbed handwriting of a functional virtue and so deprived it of its status. A new appreciation of the value and fascination that lies in writing a fair hand is rapidly arising. Teachers are discovering that the child who is brought to write well often becomes a better scholar through the enlivening and interesting practice and the self-discipline required to control the pen. The public, weary of the boredom of poor writing or perhaps conscious of the pen's excellency, is showing as much if not more creative curiosity than the schools, and the surge of interest has been enough to produce a Society for Italic Handwriting.

The views of the reforming penman of today may be summarized in this way. To take pen and write is a commonplace action. We all write and we write quickly. The pen is hurried along by driving thoughts. But words can come to the mind much more rapidly than the pen can transform them into symbols. Consequently the written words, inky trails of the rapid movements of the pen, are so frequently the awkward and inefficient products of rush and dash. There is no sense in writing, however, if what we write cannot be read. Therefore we hold in check the mind's drive on the pen for the sake of legibility. We might go farther. Just as one would wish to speak not only clearly but with some civilized and musical quality of grace, so one may write and the writing be worthy of the name of calligraphy—by which is meant handwriting considered as an art. The will to create beauty, if only in the writing of a trivial and ephemeral postcard, may override the urgency of thought and contribute another mite to the glory of life. Legibility is a product of courtesy and an aid to efficiency. Friendly correspondence is friendlier for the care and gift of graceful penmanship, and pleasure is gained both by writer and recipient when a letter is calligraphy as well as communication.

The most agreeable cursive writing we know is that which springs from the Italian Renaissance, and when considered in terms of contemporary knowledge of letter-design gives a promise of new standards. The study of fine examples of the past is recognized as a means of developing taste. For such study this book will be helpful, but the authors' prime purpose is to offer a collection of scripts as one might offer an anthology of poetry, the choice doubtless having a bearing on the history of handwriting but decided also by the authors' interest and enjoyment in these examples of the calligrapher's art, which is augmented when shared.

The Humanistic Scripts

The Italian Renaissance—that great stir in the movement of Civilization—was characterized by many features, but in particular by a fresh and freer attitude to life and an awakened interest in classical remains and models. There was an emergence from the ecclesiastical and feudal despotisms of the Middle Ages and a recognition of man as a spiritual individual. Literature and art were highly honoured. Therefore it may be regarded as natural and inevitable that the upheaval and enterprise of opinion, the passionate learning of lessons taught by Antiquity, and the enlivened interest in books, should affect the shapes of letters of the alphabet and give some new and noble contribution to calligraphy. Not only was the Gothic tradition of handwriting stemmed and a return made to an earlier and clearer tradition but the Renaissance gave us roman and italic alphabets which we accept today with very little sense of archaism, if any at all.

Petrarch (1304–74), the inaugurator and first humanist of the Italian Renaissance, was concerned to collect and preserve manuscripts, and he took pleasure in fine penmanship. In a letter to Boccaccio written in 1366 he referred to a pupil who copied letters for him in a clear hand and in contrast criticized the Gothic script of calligraphers which he found difficult to read when at hand though it was attractive at a distance. Both Petrarch and Coluccio Salutati (1330–1406), Chancellor of Florence, who is regarded as Petrarch's successor as leader of the Renaissance and founder of Florentine humanism, wrote simplified Gothic scripts that owe some clarification to Caroline influence.

The enthusiasm for the new learning gave rise to extensive searches for forgotten classic texts and to the creation of libraries by the copying of discoveries. Niccolò Niccoli (1363–1437) spent his whole fortune in buying books and collected 800 volumes. Poggio Bracciolini (1380–1459), a disciple of Coluccio and an agent of Niccoli, by industrious searches among the abbeys of south Germany and elsewhere, discovered orations of Cicero, the first complete Quintilian (covered in dust and filthy with neglect and age), and important additions to at least a dozen other classic authors. (Poggio's residence in England was not marked by equal success in his searches.) The texts were generally to be found written in Caroline scripts, and the qualities of this writing were appreciated for its clarity and simplicity and because the style was antique and in line with the spirit of humanism. Mr. E. K. Rand assumes that the Italian humanists imagined they were 'reviving the glories of their own past, unaware that they were merely repeating the achievements of the barbarians of France in a remote period of the Dark and Middle Ages'.[1]

Although the interest of humanists lay in the literature of Greece and Rome and the early Renaissance scripts were produced by its study, it is not surprising that they should show their liking for the visual appearance and easy clarity of the Caroline scripts by adopting versions of them for their own use, which they termed *lettera antiqua*. The Caroline scripts were not so far removed from Italian hands as they were from the contemporaneous scripts of England and France.

Alphabets in use in England today all derive remotely from the roman capitals. The capitals—to be seen in their most distinguished form in certain classic inscriptions carved in stone, of which that on Trajan's Column of A.D. 114 is a familiar example—were modified by the use of stylus or pen and by the simplifying effect of economy. The chisel is less suitable for making curves than the stylus or pen and the writing instruments can be used at greatly differing speeds. By various mixtures of formal and cursive influences, rustic, uncial, and half-uncial scripts were developed and the Carolingian minuscule eventually emerged. The use of the letter we know as Caroline or Carolingian was encouraged by Charlemagne and Alcuin of York at Tours and the script is a half-way house between the scripts of Roman and modern times. Many manuscripts were written in Caroline minuscules during the ninth-century renaissance, including important copies of classical Latin literature. It is held, however, that the Caroline scripts which were studied by the early Florentine humanists were probably of the tenth and eleventh centuries.

The Caroline is a hand of engaging clarity, made with many rounded strokes, but,

[1] *A Survey of the Manuscripts of Tours*, Cambridge, Mass. 1929.

in spite of having some Roman cursive blood in its veins, cursive characteristics are few. Although some ligatures occur, there is no tendency to join letters by rising diagonal strokes. The letter *m* to be seen in Plate 1 was generally made without lifting the pen—a cursive characteristic—whilst the letter *d* was possibly made with three pen-lifts—a formal characteristic.

Early Humanistic Scripts

The revival of bookhands in the Caroline tradition had begun in the early years of the fifteenth century. In his essay: *Early Humanistic Script and the First Roman Type,*[1] Mr. Stanley Morison shows several scripts written by Niccoli and Poggio. The disciplined script of Poggio Bracciolini is humanistic (roman) but all the six scripts attributed to Niccoli by Mr. Morison have diagonal joins and though they vary in discipline and speed they may be thought of for this reason as humanistic cursives (italic, more or less). The diagonal join (the thin connecting upstroke made by a sideways movement of the pen) was used before the Renaissance in certain medieval scripts. It is a natural agent of currency and a break-away from the formality of making letters by pulled strokes fitted together. Speed and economy introduce the upstroke and that movement certainly is the power which produced the essential italic shapes. Although one may point to many fine italic scripts where, say, the letter *n* is made of two strokes (i.e. with an interior pen-lift), yet the characteristic shape of an italic *n* comes essentially from an upstroke.

Niccoli, one of a circle associated with the elder Cosimo de' Medici, was a handsome man of sensitive spirit and kindly speech, a perfectionist, a bibliophile, and a collector of antiques such as ancient vases and crystal goblets, a friend of scholars and artists, an inspirer of young men, and a promoter of the copying of manuscripts. This passionate scholar and gifted penman, Mr. Morison considers 'was more responsible than any of his contemporaries for the trend taken by humanistic calligraphy', and it may be that he was the first italic writer. Niccoli was assisted at one time in his search for manuscripts by Tommaso Parentucelli of Sarzana, who became Nicholas V and whose vast collection of manuscripts formed the foundation of the Vatican Library.

[1] *The Library*, 4th series, vol. xxiv, 1943, Nos. 1 and 2. There is doubt felt now as to the authenticity of attributions to Niccoli of certain of these scripts, but the hand shown in Plate 2 is not questioned (except for its quality as a script!).

The bookhand of Poggio's best period is regarded by Mr. Morison as representing the most highly developed form of the humanistic (roman) script. His earliest roman script precedes in date Niccoli's italic.

The copying of manuscripts became a notable feature: Federigo, Duke of Urbino, kept thirty or forty *scrittori* employed in various places; and Vespasiano, with forty-five writers under him, delivered to Cosimo de' Medici 200 volumes in twenty-two months. The *scrittori* were professional copyists who generally understood Greek. Others called *copisti* included schoolmasters and needy men of learning, who desired an addition to their income.[1] Vespasiano da Bisticci is known to have provided English scholars with manuscripts, namely William de Grey, Bishop of Ely, John Tiptoft, Earl of Worcester, and Andrew Holes. Manuscripts copied by the famous calligraphers Antonio di Mario and Gherardo del Ciriago, who worked for Vespasiano, are in Balliol College, Oxford.

Mr. John P. Elder has divided Florentine humanistic manuscripts into three periods,[2] the transitional (1375–1425), in which the scribes laboriously and often unsuccessfully strive to forsake their Gothic ways for older ones; the middle (1425–65), in which they develop their new script, so that at once it strikingly suggests Carolingian models yet displays such uneasy artificiality as one might expect from scribes who are still far from at home with the new medium and are keeping one wary eye on their 'model alphabet'; and finally the perfected (1465–90), in which the copyists have so easily and comfortably mastered the 'feel' of this part-Carolingian, part-Gothic script that a distinctly new type of writing has been created. The representative Florentine professional scribes and outstanding masters of these three periods, writing roman hands, were Antonio di Mario, Gherardo del Ciriago, and Antonio Sinibaldi.

Humanistic Cursives

The humanistic cursive (italic), at first an informal hand, because of its very informality did not find at once the status which it achieved later. Niccoli had at the outset adapted the Caroline script by modifying the letter forms to conform to the introduction of joins and suitable upstrokes and he had thus created an italic system, but it took many years to learn the lesson that the humanistic cursive could be developed and refined to take on a new and superb form. Roughly, the Caroline

---

[1] *The Civilisation of the Renaissance in Italy*, by Jacob Burckhardt.
[2] 'Clues for Dating Florentine Humanistic Manuscripts', *Studies in Philology*, vol. xliv, April 1947, No. 2.

minuscule can be said to relate to the circle but the italic to the ellipse. The circle is linked to formality but the ellipse tends more to informality and quick movements of the pen. (Cf. Arrighi's opinion given in note to Plates 57 to 59.) The 'eye-charming form of an oval', which Edward Cocker recognized, is not inferior in grace to the quietness and clarity of the circle. It was inevitable that the cursive letter, so different and yet so near to the roman letter, should be refined and elevated in standing and eventually achieve distinction of form, since Renaissance penmen were interested in the design of letters. Perhaps it is not irrelevant to remark that obviously it requires greater skill to write rapidly with distinction than to write slowly. Often we find bookhands of the fifteenth century that are neither purely formal nor informal, and which seem not to have accepted the upstroke as the dominating cursive factor which shapes and tends to narrow the letter. For contrasts of scripts it is interesting to compare the delicate roman hand of Marcus de Cribellariis of Vicenza, well known from being illustrated in the numerous editions of Edward Johnston's *Writing & Illuminating, & Lettering*, namely in Plate XX of that book, with the equally delightful hand illustrated in plate 4. Without doubt, Mark of Vicenza was pleased with the traces left by his flying pen (*calamo volanti*).

The humanistic cursives used in the manuscript books of the late fifteenth century are various. The stabilizing influence of printing could have less effect on italic letter forms than on the *lettera antiqua,* since it was not until 1501 that the first italic type was used, whilst Jenson's noble roman appeared in 1470. But it is conceivable and likely that the interest in the classic inscriptions cut in roman capitals which was notable about 1460, and, later, in their geometrical proportions, would have directed some attention also to the design of minuscules, both formal and informal. Certainly by the turn of the century the best of humanistic cursives can be said to be good and sensitive in form, expressive of quick rhythmical and disciplined movements, and worthy of regard as mature scripts. Printing or some other formalizing influence had not yet tended to eliminate the diagonal joins, noticeably absent from the scripts displayed in Plates 40 and 41. Plate 11 shows a script which seems to be written by the same person who wrote the 'semi-formal' hand that has excited so many of the readers of Edward Johnston's book, and who, James Wardrop thought, may have been a papal scribe.[1] Among other skilful writers in italic who have been the subject of Mr. Wardrop's studies were Pierantonio Sallando[2] and Bartolomeo Sanvito of Padua (1435–?1518) (Plates 8 and 9).

---

[1] *Six Italian Manuscripts in the Department of Graphic Arts,* by James Wardrop.
[2] *Pierantonio Sallando and Girolamo Pagliarolo,* by James Wardrop.

Documents in Italic Hands

Humanistic cursive in the fifteenth century was not confined to the making of manuscript books: it became a diplomatic hand and one used by scholars and artists. About the middle of the century it was adopted by Eugenius IV for the writing of papal briefs, and from this use was later described by Arrighi as *littera cancellarescha*. A number of these briefs addressed to Henry VIII and Wolsey are in the British Museum and Public Record Office.[1] They are written on parchment wide enough to contain very long lines of writing, which may be as much as 18 inches and with over thirty words to a line, yet the text may be contained in as few as three lines. The difficulty of introducing into books facsimiles of such awkward-sized and often decayed documents has meant that the public who knows that briefs were written in italics is unaware of their appearance. We have the pleasure not only of reproducing two briefs but also in our belief that Arrighi probably wrote them (Plates 16 and 17). Certainty in this attribution awaits further supporting evidence.

Surprise may be felt that so refined a version of Arrighi's cancellaresca, worthy of one who might be thought of as one of his best pupils, should have been written in London (Plate 21). It is fascinating to see Henry VIII's well-designed and regal but medieval signature heading a letter looking so Italian in its italic competence and style (Plate 22). Further, the letter from the King of Poland has an Italian appearance. As to the spread of italic, the author has noticed a fine italic script written in January 1518 by Passamonte and addressed to Catherine of Aragon from Sanctodomingo and he wonders if there can be earlier italic writing issuing from America.[2]

The handwriting of artists of the Renaissance naturally engages one's attention. The three hands illustrated in Plates 13, 38, and 39, of Raphael, Michael Angelo, and Cellini are in vivid contrast. Raphael's skilful pen moves in sensitive and exquisite motions, Michael Angelo's script has something of the disciplined form of a poem, and Cellini writes as one can imagine he talked.

Writing Manuals

The spread of learning created a demand for instruction in handwriting, and numerous writing manuals were produced during the sixteenth century. The first,

---

[1] Parts of two briefs not reproduced here are included in *A Handwriting Manual*, by Alfred Fairbank. They show variations in the script inevitable in cursive handwriting but indicating also that there was not a rigid standard in the Papal Chancery.   [2] Public Record Office, S.P. 1/16, f. 106.

a book which is sometimes claimed to be the most beautiful of all writing-books, was produced by Ludovico Arrighi Vicentino in Rome in 1522. *La Operina di Ludovico Vicentino, da imparare di scrivere littera Cancellarescha*, a book of thirty-two pages printed from wood-blocks engraved by Ugo di Carpi shows the *littera corsiva* or *cancellarescha* for the benefit of Arrighi's friends and with a prophetic eye to posterity. A year later Arrighi published a second writing book, *Il modo de temperare le penne*, which included an example of *litera da brevi* amongst other alphabets and scripts. The preparation of this book began in Rome but it was printed in Venice in 1523 in association with Eustachio Celebrino.

Arrighi was not only a professional scribe and writer of apostolic briefs, but a publisher, printer, and type-designer. His experience and his knowledge of the motions appropriate to a fast handwriting and of what is required of an alphabet contributed to his success as a teacher. The writing-master must be analytical and simplify his teaching, for latitude is not what the pupil needs at the beginning of instruction. Some standardization and precise rules are to be noted in *La Operina*, but it is pleasing to find in Arrighi the sympathetic teacher who realizes that it may be impossible to keep to a rule concerning spacing and who leaves another matter, to tie or not to tie letters, to the judgement of the learner. Proverbs are a common feature of copy-books: Arrighi writes as an exemplar *che vale in campo intrare, et poi fuggire?* (Why enter the field of battle and then flee?)

Arrighi's work as a book-scribe is known. James Wardrop drew attention to Arrighi's illuminated manuscript *Aristotelis Ethica*, now in the possession of the Universiteits Bibliotheek, Amsterdam, which was completed at Rome in October 1517 and was probably intended for Vittoria Colonna, that famous and impressive Italian woman, the friend of Michael Angelo and Castiglione. Two other manuscript books probably written by Arrighi have since come to light in England. Of these, the finer is one of the manuscripts of the Royal Library in the British Museum, which the author had the good fortune to come upon in his searches: namely the copy of the *Apologues* of Pandolfo Collenuccio, &c. presented to Henry VIII by Geoffrey Chamber (cf. Mr. Wolpe's notes and Plates 60 and 61). The other is a Book of Hours which is on view in the Fitzwilliam Museum, Cambridge, and is represented in Plate 62a. There are also fragments, dismaying and yet fascinating, in the British Museum of G. G. Trissino's *Sophonisba* (Plate 62b). All these books are written in set italic, with hardly a diagonal join to be seen.

The third writing-book to show the cancellaresca hand is that of Giovanantonio Tagliente, *Opera che insegna a scrivere*, which first appeared in 1524 in Venice (after thirty-two years of teaching) but ran into numerous editions, at least thirty. An italic hand, graceful and of sensitive touch, written by Tagliente in 1491 is in a supplication to the Doge and Council of Venice for a convenient stipend so that he may live with his family in Venice, in respect of which he offers to teach and instruct cancellarescha to the young men dedicated to the Chancery, without other expense (Plate 65a).[1] His published models include various mercantile hands, *lettera antiqua tonda, lettera formata, lettera bollatica,* &c. but he exploited a number of his italic models for the display of his ability to decorate a script by intricate ligatures and flourishes. The examples in Plate 65b, not spoiled by convolutions but too pointed for our liking, do show his considerable skill as a letter-designer, and particularly his acceptance of the dominating hairline upstroke. The difference between the two scripts, for example, proceeds from a difference in the angle of the hairline, the upstroke of the lower example ascending at a steeper angle than in the piece above. Mr. James M. Wells has drawn attention to various manuals compiled by Tagliente, including a pattern-book for lace and embroidery, and suggests that Tagliente's interest in applied decoration and his skill at it, influenced his calligraphy.[2] Tagliente was helped in the production of his writing-book by his son Pietro. Some, at least, of his models were engraved by Eustachio Celebrino.

Giovanbattista Palatino was a native of Rossano in Calabria and a citizen of Rome. He was prominent in intellectual circles and the Secretary of the Accademia dei Sdegnati. James Wardrop wrote about him with much sympathy[3] and he regarded him as one of the most deservedly popular, accomplished, and versatile of Renaissance scribes. Indeed, he termed him the 'calligrapher's calligrapher' and claimed that had he not lived 'Queen Elizabeth, and Bartholomew Dodington; Esther Inglis & William Alabaster (to name a few only among the most admired of English penmen) had not written as they did'. This statement may be true but it was made before the influence in England of Tagliente's earlier manual and of Sir John Cheke had been appreciated.

Palatino's writing-book *Libro nuovo d'imparare a scrivere,* first published in Rome in 1540, enlarged in 1545, and revised in 1566, displayed many scripts, but his principal model was the *lettere Cancellarescha.* Mr. Wardrop gave him considerable credit for his *Cancellarescha Formata* (Plate 70b). Palatino's cursive, remarkable for its unity and for this reason supporting Mr. Wardrop's comment that Palatino's attitude to writing

---

[1] 'A Note on Giovanantonio Tagliente', by James Wardrop. *Signature,* No. 8, N.S.
[2] *Opera di Giovanniantonio Tagliente,* reproduced in facsimile with an introduction by James M. Wells.
[3] *Civis Romanus Sum: Giovanbattista Palatino and his Circle,* by James Wardrop.

was transcendental, is undoubtedly somewhat unsympathetically received today because of its narrow, compacted, pointed, Gothic, and excessively disciplined characteristics, and is considered hardly suitable as a contemporary model for the development of a free cursive. Arrighi's exemplars had not been improved upon by Palatino. But it has at least one virtue as a model, for the spacing of letters in the narrow words is most skilfully organized.

Plate 70a shows his *testa*, *traverso*, and *taglio*, three principal strokes of the alphabet. Arrighi's instructions in *La Operina* open with the making of two strokes, one flat and thick and the other acute and thin (related, of course, to Palatino's *testa* and *taglio*) with either of which the *cancellaresca* letters begin. Palatino is surprised that those who have described the ways and means of writing (presumably Arrighi is in his mind) had not mentioned the second stroke (*traverso*). Of these three strokes he remarks, in effect, that the relationship of thickness of stroke is as five (*testa*) is to four (*traverso*) is to one (*taglio*). This is not more than to say that an edged pen is used which is held in such a way that the thinnest stroke is at 45 degrees to the horizontal.

Another important writing-book which appeared in numerous editions is by a Franciscan, Vespasiano Amphiareo, namely *Opera nella quale si insegna a scrivere*, published in Venice in 1554. His exemplars of both *lettra bastarda* and *cancellaresche* show a sturdy and elegant letter, practically upright, narrow and yet curvilinear, engraved with sympathetic skill. The diagonal join, though not absent from the models, is not a significant feature, and therefore one cannot think of it as a potentially fast script, though ligatures borrowed from mercantile hands now appear. The virtue of his italic exemplars is in the musical patterning and spacing, the graceful assembly of well-designed units, and the appropriate reticence of ornament and display. Two manuscripts of Vespasiano's are in Harvard College Library[1] and Plate 75 is from one of them.

The example in Plate 67 from Ferdinando Ruano's *Sette Alphabeti* (Rome, 1554) is included with a warning that Ruano must not be judged by this interesting extravagance, for James Wardrop has shown his *cancellarescha formata* to be a fine and graceful hand and the scripts in Plates 42 and 43 are written in his style.[2] Since letters seem often to be related to the circle, the ellipse, the rectangle, the arch, and the angle, and their essential form is a matter of proportion, it is not surprising that some letterers should be attracted to geometrical construction, irrespective of the fact that the Renaissance aroused a general interest in geometrical and human proportions.

---

[1] *Six Italian Manuscripts in the Department of Graphic Arts*, by James Wardrop.
[2] 'The Vatican Scriptors: Documents for Ruano and Cresci', by James Wardrop. *Signature*, No. 5, N.S., 1948.

What is surprising is that the gradations, notably in *d*, are not exactly such as an edged pen would make. Ruano, a Spaniard, was a *Scrittore latino* at the Vatican Library from 1541 until his death in 1560.

Giovanni Francesco Cresci, regarded as the first calligrapher of the Baroque, became a Scriptor in the Vatican Library in 1556. He fiercely criticized what is thought to be the model of Palatino as being slow and heavy and without delight or quickness because it is too pointed and he blamed the oblique hold of the too-broad and too-squarely cut pen. When he states that he holds his pen nearly straight there is an indication at once of the decline of *cancellaresca*. The motions of the hand which shaped italic are not those appropriate to the use of a straight pen. Cresci was right to accent the virtues of a somewhat rounded letter and the use of joins, and if he liked a pen cut much closer in the point and somewhat more rounded than usual, so probably did many other Renaissance calligraphers. Whilst we are considering his credits we must remark that his alphabet of roman capitals[1] is one of the best of all alphabets, yet to recommend the straight pen and a greater slant in writing was regrettable. The straight pen (presumably pointing to the shoulder) is that suitable to writing with regulated pressures, as in copperplate.

. The writing-book of Giuliantonio Hercolani, published in Bologna in 1574, introduces a new and influential method of reproducing models: i.e. by printing from engraved copperplates. This method eventually led to a natural decadence in handwriting, for the engraver's tool does not operate as does the pen used for the earlier cursives and the gradations cannot easily be copied by a pen. Engraving is performed mirror-wise and the reversed letters are made by scratchings and incisions. The engraved alphabets are often quite charming and perfectly suitable as models for engravers, but the pen should be master of its own house, and produce its own standards. Writing-masters today are at an advantage since their exemplars may be reproduced by photographic methods, and therefore the pen, and not the engraver's tool, can be the guide to penmanship.

In the last quarter of the sixteenth century there were many manuals published in Italy.[2]

Scripts having such conspicuous virtues as humanistic and italic hands would naturally excite attention wherever they were seen, whether in copies of the classics or in diplomatic documents, and would march with the New Learning. The demand for instruction in writing the *cancellaresca* hand was met outside Italy by various

[1] Plates 30 and 31 of *A Book of Scripts*.
[2] 'A Catalogue of Italian Writing Books of the Sixteenth Century', by A. F. Johnson. *Signature*, No. 10, N.S.

sixteenth-century writing-books, of which those that attract the authors most are by Mercator, Yciar, Lucas, and de Beauchesne.

Literarum Latinarum . . . Ratio, produced in Antwerp in 1540 by Mercator, the famous geographer, plainly indicates how impressed was its author by the importance of the diagonal join and the hairline upstroke. The book shows a rugged letter, which has doubtless suffered from its conversion to a print from a wood-block, but the script is clear enough to illustrate intention and it gives a forward movement, whilst the flourishes add to the sense of handwriting being a dance of the pen. The instruction in writing the hand is more detailed than that of Arrighi (Plates 71 to 73).

The books of the three Spanish writing-masters show brilliant exemplars. Juan de Yciar praises Arrighi, Tagliente, and Palatino, in his *Arte Subtilissima* (Saragossa, 1555) and is known to have come under Palatino's personal influence when a youth in Italy, as one can guess from the tight and pointed models engraved by Juan de Vingles. Francisco Lucas displays exquisite pieces, free of the angularity of Palatino's *cancellarescha*, in his *Arte de escrevir* (Madrid, 1577), and but for a failure to include the diagonal join as an essential feature of the script (on the rare occasions when in use it tends to come awkwardly) they would be most excellent models. By engraving the wood-block so that only the letters are cut away, the engraver gives a more precise and brilliant representation of the play of thicks, thins, and gradations. The bland flattened curves and the elegant proportions of the letters, the rhythmical spacing, the serenity and unity of the inscriptions enlivened by flourishes kept well under control, are features which are immediately apprehended (Plates 78 to 84).

A facsimile of the two rare writing-books of Andres Brun of Saragossa (dated 1583 and 1612) was produced by the Pegasus Press of Paris in 1928, from which our illustration was drawn (Plate 85).

Spain enjoyed a revival of italic handwriting in the eighteenth century: two notable writing-books published in Madrid were those of Palomares and Servidori.

Italic Handwriting in England

Italic was slow in establishing a position in England, where the ordinary hand of the sixteenth century was Secretary, and for long after its introduction it was used to but a small extent, even by the learned. At first and for a considerable time italic was the hand of the travelled, of the Court, and of the universities. Sir Hilary Jenkinson has observed that the first italic signatures in the Common Paper of the Scriveners'

Company began in 1554 and that by this time men of university standing and the professional writers would learn it as well as the Secretary hand, 'but for another century it remained, even for scholars, the writing of ceremony'.[1]

Secretary was regarded as more rapid than the Elizabethan italic. Martin Billingsley describes it in 1618 as 'the onely usuall hand of England for dispatching of all manner of business', but he also refers to the Italian hand 'which of late is growne very usuall and is much affected'.[2] The two hands were sometimes mixed and in various ways. In a letter in Secretary, italic might be used for emphasis or for a quotation, as the printer now uses it, but italic letters might be introduced into the hand or the letter might be signed in italic.

The pointed Elizabethan italic is a beautiful script and truly a superb hand when written by Dodington, yet it generally lacks the economy of movements that give currency. This deficiency did not bring forth a more current curvilinear English model, and this presumably is due to the available alternative which Secretary was regarded as providing.

Eventually the italic influence became predominant. Owing much to the teaching and copperplate models of European writing-masters (Lucas Materot, Jan van den Velde, Louis Barbedor, Ambrosius Perlingh, &c.) italic changed into the copperplate of England's thriving business of the eighteenth century and found its way back to the Continent as *Anglaise*.

Since italic is a product of the Renaissance it is fitting to remark that Richard de Bury (1281–1345), Bishop of Durham, Tutor, Treasurer, and Chancellor of Edward III, and author of *Philobiblon*, was imbued with the chief ideas of humanism, and had met Petrarch at Avignon. He was one of the first bibliophiles in Europe and is known to have searched monastic libraries and to have rescued manuscripts from destruction. But neither he nor Poggio, who, during his residence in England from 1418 to 1422, searched for manuscripts and was corresponding with Niccolò Niccoli can be shown to have directly affected English handwriting.

It has been observed already that many manuscripts written in the humanistic *littera antiqua* reached England in the fifteenth century. William de Grey, Bishop of Ely (d. 1478), the first Englishman to attend the lectures of Guarino da Verona at Ferrara, gave manuscripts, including works copied by the famous calligrapher Antonio di Mario, to Balliol College.

The credit for being the first to introduce humanistic cursive into England is given traditionally to Petrus Carmelianus, a native of Brescia who was born about

[1] *The Later Court Hands in England*, by Sir Hilary Jenkinson.   [2] *The Pen's Excellencie.*

the middle of the fifteenth century, came to England probably in 1480, and who died in 1527. He was a poet who became Latin Secretary to Henry VII, lute-player to Henry VIII, and prebendary of York (Plates 6 and 14). One may hazard that the traditional credit relates to the use of the hand at Court. In the Register of Oxford University[1] an entry dated 1449 was made in a sloped Roman hand written too fast to preserve its set form and taking on something of the character of italic. In this Register may be seen also an entry of 1459 written and signed by John Farley (who died in 1464) in a rapid hand that is predominantly a humanistic cursive. An unsigned entry dated 1470 is nearer to the later conception of italic.

The New Learning was not much favoured by Henry VII and was represented by but a few scholars during his reign. The sympathies of Henry VIII (1491–1547) who ascended the throne in 1509, were, however, with the new order, and throughout his reign his home was a home of letters. Many Greek scholars had fled to the shores of Italy after the capture of Constantinople in 1453 and foreign scholars journeyed to Italy to learn Greek from them. About 1485 Thomas Linacre, the friend of Grocyn, Latimer, and Colet, and who later was the founder and first president of the College of Physicians, was allowed by Lorenzo de' Medici to share instruction in Greek given in Florence by Poliziano and the exile Chalcondylas to the two young princes, Piero and Giovanni de' Medici. The latter became Pope Leo X and his election seemed to give to the New Learning the control of Christendom. In 1523, a year before his death, Linacre was Latin tutor to Princess Mary.

Other Latin Secretaries to Henry VIII who wrote an italic hand were Andrea Ammonio of Lucca (1477–1517) and Peter Vannes (d. 1563) who was probably a relative of Ammonio. Vannes had an assistant whose fine hand is often to be found in the State Papers of Henry VIII and is shown in Plate 24 of *A Book of Scripts*.

Another at the Court of Henry VIII was Johannes Mallard, who wrote both roman and italic bookhands and who, in an illuminated manuscript book with miniatures of Henry VIII and marginal comments in Henry's hand, describes himself as *regius orator & a calamo*.[2]

Among the tutors of the children of Henry VIII who themselves wrote an italic hand were Richard Croke, Sir John Cheke, and Roger Ascham. A natural son of Henry VIII and Elizabeth Blount, namely Henry Fitzroy, Duke of Richmond and Somerset, was a pupil of Richard Croke for a time and the boy's writing then followed that of this master. (Plate 24 shows an astonishing performance for a boy of seven

[1] University Archives, Oxford, Register F.4.   [2] British Museum, Royal 2 A XVI.

years of age and it is matched by another[1] letter in somewhat similar terms to his father, probably written on the same day—4 March 1526.)

The letter of Queen Katharine Parr written in an italic hand (Plate 29) is amusing for its calligraphical decoration, and it raises the question as to who influenced her to write so. The question is partly answered by the fact that there are signs in the letter of study of Tagliente's manual. It is interesting to compare this letter with that of Elizabeth (Plate 28) written years later.

Although the first centre of humanism at the universities was at Oxford, later Cambridge became more influential through a brilliant company of scholars whose leader was Cheke.

In his *Life of Sir John Cheke* (1702), John Strype states: '. . . he brought in fair and graceful writing by the pen, as he wrote an excellent, accurate hand himself. And all the best scholars in those times practised to write well. So did Smith and Cecil, and especially Ascham; who, for his exquisite hand, was the person appointed to teach the Lady Elizabeth to write. So that fair writing and good learning seemed to commence together.' Although it can hardly be said that Cheke brought in fair writing, this may refer to his influence at Cambridge and at Court, which must have been considerable. Cheke was a reformer and held views on Greek pronunciation, Latin orthography, the use of English, and the spelling of English words. Like Ascham, he wrote several versions of the italic hand, one of which had certain letters of the alphabet not belonging to traditional italic. This script, which I call the 'Cheke hand', is to be seen in Plate 27, whilst Dodington's more precise version of it is shown in Plate 47. The 'Cheke hand' was written also (and more or less) by Roger Ascham, John Becon, Roger Brown, Bartholomew Clerk, John Cocks, Robert Johnson, William Lewin, William Mount, Edward Seymer, &c., but the fashion eventually died out, leaving no noted result. The introduced letters, of which ẟ (d) is a conspicuous example, offer no immediate explanation of their significance, but other features, namely the up-and-down strokes of ascenders, the greater continuity of strokes, and the tendency to curves in such letters as *b*, *h*, *m*, and *n*, suggest speed and currency. Another feature making for economy, to be seen in many later examples of the 'Cheke hand', is the small size of the writing. Cheke's views on spelling reform are given by Strype but the introduced letters do not appear to be phonetic symbols.

Ascham referred to Cheke in *The Scholemaster* as 'the Ientleman of worthie memorie, my dearest frend, and teacher of all the little poore learning I haue, Syr Iohn Cheke'.

---

[1] Public Record Office, S.P. I/Vol. 37.

Cheke was an oral teacher, not famous for any printed work. Both Cheke and Ascham were Greek scholars and both held the post of Public Orator at Cambridge. Cheke's favourite pupil is said by Sir John Neale to have been Ascham, and Ascham's to have been William Grindall. William Cecil, afterwards Lord Burghley, married Cheke's sister Mary. Cheke was not only tutor to Edward VI but had occasionally acted as tutor to Princess Elizabeth and through him Ascham had made the acquaintance of the future queen. On Cheke's advice William Grindall was brought to Court in 1544, when Elizabeth was eleven years of age, to be her tutor and Ascham gave him advice on his teaching. When Grindall died of the plague in 1548, Ascham became her tutor at her wish and in spite of Henry's widow, Katharine Parr, and Admiral Seymour, pressing the claims of another, named Goldsmith. Ascham's handwriting had brought him employment as the writer of official letters from Cambridge University.[1]

When Elizabeth was eleven years old she was writing with some skill an italic bookhand of Italian appearance. This script can be seen in two manuscript books. The earlier book, in the Bodleian Library, is *The Glasse* (or *Mirror*) *of the Synneful Soule*, a translation by Elizabeth from the French of Queen Margaret of Navarre, and it was offered to Queen Katharine Parr on 31 December 1544.[2] The second book, at the British Museum, of *Prayers and Meditations* composed by Queen Katharine Parr, was presented to her father a year later.[3]

Ascham had had influence on her penmanship before as well as during his tutorship, which was chiefly at Cheshunt from 1548 to 1550.[4] His admiration for Elizabeth's handwriting is well known. Even as late as 1562, when Elizabeth had been a queen for four years, Ascham had sent to his friend Sturm a slip of paper with the word *quemadmodum* written in the Queen's hand and had asked Sturm to say whether the sight was pleasant to him.

When Latin Secretary to Mary (he was specially permitted to continue in his profession of protestantism), Ascham is said to have written forty-seven letters for Mary to persons of exalted rank, of whom cardinals were the lowest, within three days.[5] (Not all of such letters were written with much precision, for he often wrote a rapid italic hand with a dominating use of joins.) Another interesting incident is that before

[1] Two of these are in the volume S.P. 1/214 at the Public Record Office.
[2] MS. Cherry 36.   [3] Royal 7. D. X.
[4] Ascham reports in *The Scholemaster* that Sir Richard Sackville said to him: '. . . seeing God did so blesse you, to make you the Scholer of the best Master, and also the Scholemaster of the best Scholer, that ever were in our tyme . . .'.
[5] A number of drafts written in 1556 by Ascham are in S.P. 11/9 at the Public Record Office.

he was appointed Elizabeth's tutor he sent a silver pen to Mrs. Ashley, her governess, as a token and offered to mend Elizabeth's silver pen. Ascham gave lessons in penmanship also to Edward VI,[1] to the young Lords, Henry and Charles Brandon, who died in 1551, and to Rudolph Ratcliffe.

The quintessence of the Cambridge tradition of English italic is to be seen in the letter shown in Plate 46 which undoubtedly was written by Bartholomew Dodington (1536–95). Dodington became a Regius Professor of Greek at Cambridge, and as the illustration indicates, he, like Ascham, wrote official letters for the university. He was also an Auditor of the Imprest and his exquisite signature appears surprisingly on a warrant for the transfer of certain munitions from the Tower to Chester. For a period of at least twenty-nine years Dodington wrote the very controlled pointed italic of Plate 46 (shown also in Plate 27 of *A Book of Scripts*) but he also wrote the faster and freer 'Cheke hand'—sometimes exceedingly small—and this practice may have contributed a lightening effect on the severe angularity of the set script. Strype states that Dodington was a companion of Sir John Cheke's eldest son Henry: Dodington was twelve years older than Henry Cheke. Dodington may not have had direct contact with Sir John Cheke but the calligraphical relationship of Cheke, Ascham, and Dodington is established by an inscription in a printed book[2] in the library of St. John's College, Cambridge, which shows that it was given by Roger Ascham, a generous man, to Dodington in 1566: i.e. when Ascham was fifty-one years of age and Dodington thirty.

A vast number of documents exists addressed to or dealt with by Lord Burghley, and among them is a considerable amount of writing by Cecil himself which can be said to make up in nervous energy what it lacks in clarity. His early writing, presumably that which impressed Strype, was probably very good but has not come yet to the notice of the author, but the shadows of Burghley's interest in handwriting are clearly seen not only in the quality of the writing of many of the letters of ceremony he received from Cambridge and the coaxing requests for favours from individuals but also in such circumstances as that at least three excellent writers of italic were in his service: Thomas Windebanke was companion to his eldest son, Thomas, who became Earl of Exeter, William Lewin taught a daughter, and William Mount is thought to have been his domestic chaplain. Several of Dodington's letters

---

[1] In a letter to Stephen Gardiner, written at the end of 1553, Ascham states 'I was sent for many times to teach the king to write, and brought him before a xi years old to write as fair a hand, though I say it, as any child in England, as a letter in his own hand doth declare, which I kept as a treasure for a witness of my service. . . .'   [2] *Caroli Sigoni de Rep. Atheniensium*, Venice, 1565.

were addressed to him and his daughter's 'bade writynge' shown in Plate 54 is also evidence. Moreover, it is relevant that Peter Bales, who won a golden pen of twenty pounds in a writing match with Daniel Johnson in 1595, applied to Burghley (? in 1591) to accept him into his lordship's 'Honorable service this Newyeares daye for a poore Newyeares gift'.[1]

Petruccio Ubaldini (1524?–1600?) was a scholar and penman born in Tuscany who came to England in 1545 and was employed in the service of the Crown. He copied and illuminated manuscripts, taught Italian, and translated tracts. There are a number of specimen books, other than those illustrated, in the British Museum and elsewhere, written more or less in the style of the printed writing-books, namely by J. Delahay, Esther Inglis, Francesco Alumno, William Teshe, John Scottowe, which might well engage the attention of a scholar.

The first writing-book printed in England appeared in 1570, namely *A Booke Containing Divers Sortes of Hands*, made by John de Beauchesne in association with John Baildon. Mr. Berthold Wolpe has made a study of Beauchesne and promises a book about this writing-master with a facsimile of his manual. Beauchesne may have written the charming italic example in *The Petie Schole* by Francis Clement.[2]

Many fine scripts clamoured for inclusion in the plates of this book, and the authors confess to having yielded to the charming appeal or spectacular showmanship of several of the examples and to have rejected, though regretfully, more sober pieces in their favour. To John Palmer, a student of Trinity College, Cambridge, and later Archdeacon of Ely, who uses gold in his epistolary blandishments, are added Captain Wybrandt Bornstra, who encloses the letter illustrated in Plate 53 as a supplement to a long narrative in which he boasts of his services to the Queen and complains of ill treatment, Dr. John Dee, another Cambridge Fellow, a mathematician and astrologer who at the time his letter was written was the head of a small confraternity for seeking the philosopher's stone and invoking the angels, and Arabella Stuart, whose miserable circumstances are well known.

We should also have liked to include examples from the pens of Thomas Winter, Anthony Jebb, George Gascoigne, Charles Yetsweart, Robert Walter, William Whitaker, William Chaderton, Peter Bales, and others which we have noticed and admired. To our regret the rejection of many fine pieces has excluded hands written at Oxford University, where the Italian influence is often more noticeable in a compacted curvilinear letter than in the angular italic of Cambridge.

---

[1] Lansdown 99, art. 102.   [2] Plate 35 of *A Book of Scripts*.

The Contemporary Revival of Italic Handwriting

Two notable calligraphic movements of this century have started in England and have spread and taken roots overseas. Another impressive movement was begun in Germany by the teaching of Rudolf Koch. The first English school, springing from the practice and teaching of Edward Johnston (1872–1944), has produced in this country so many professional calligraphers from amongst his pupils and their pupils that since 1921 there has been an active Society of Scribes and Illuminators aiming to re-establish a tradition of craftsmanship in the production of manuscripts. This Society, recognizing the widespread interest arising in italic handwriting and the need for another Society to satisfy the requirements of teachers and amateurs, inaugurated the Society for Italic Handwriting in November 1952, which rapidly collected a large membership from many countries.

The recognition of the virtues of the humanistic cursives of the fifteenth and sixteenth centuries has spread rapidly since the Second World War but appreciation of these scripts began many years ago. In the early seventies of last century William Morris, who possessed a volume in which were bound four calligraphical items (two of Arrighi, one of Tagliente, and one of Fanti), was making manuscript books, written in italic as well as in other scripts, and these were shown to the public at the first exhibition of the Arts and Crafts Exhibition Society in 1888. Another poet, Robert Bridges, at the time of his marriage in 1884 shared an interest in hand-writing with his young wife. Mrs. M. M. Bridges, whose great-grandfather was John Hodgkin (1766–1845), a writing-master and the author of *Calligraphia Graeca et Poecilographia Graeca* and two other works on penmanship, a few weeks after her marriage was seeking to borrow from Lionel Muirhead a *Petrarch* for a model alphabet to use in copying matter for her husband. In 1898 she issued her book *The New Handwriting* at the insistence of teachers and showed models influenced by her acquaintance with the 'Italianized Gothic of the sixteenth century'. The inclusion of illustrations of two superb italic scripts in the numerous editions of Edward John-ston's *Writing & Illuminating, & Lettering*, namely from a book of Bembo's poems written in 1543 and now in the Victoria and Albert Museum and from a book of epigraphic inscriptions, has shown the world of lettering two heights of italic grace, but they seem too steep to climb. Graily Hewitt, who was advised by Sir Sydney Cockerell to become one of Johnston's pupils, produced the *Oxford Copy-books* in 1916, but his fine italic script ot that period had no joins. The author was taught formal calligraphy by Graily Hewitt and Lawrence Christie and found much interest in bookhands but later more in informal italic writing. In addition to his books and exemplars there are a number of other publications relating to the teaching of italic handwriting. There have also been notable historical researches by such devoted scholars as the late James Wardrop, Mr. A. F. Johnson, Mr. Stanley Morison, Professor B. L. Ullman, and Mr. Berthold Wolpe, who have recovered much lost knowledge of Renaissance calligraphy and its practitioners and exemplars.

It is not assumed that Arrighi considered his simplified and standardized models suitable for very young children, but there is now ample proof that the further simplification of the humanistic cursive as in the *Dryad Writing Cards*, and coupled with appropriate pens, has made the system suitable for children of eight years of age and over. Indeed, infants can and do write italic with pencil and chalk, and the author has written two copy-books (*Beacon Writing Books* I and II) in collaboration with Miss Charlotte Stone for the teaching of the beginnings of italic handwriting in schools, on the principle that one should start as one means to go on. It is held by the author that no simpler alphabet could be offered.

Capitals

The capital letters of the humanistic cursives derive from the ancestor of all of our English lettering of today: the classic roman capitals. Three versions of capitals are in evidence in Renaissance calligraphy. First, the rather simple capitals that come from the study of Caroline manuscripts which are to be seen in Plates 2 and 3; then, from about 1460, the carefully and skilfully formed capitals springing directly from the authority of the classic Roman inscriptions; and finally, a reaction from the influence of the chisel and towards the freedom of the pen, the flourished 'swash' capitals.

The study of the classic Roman capitals found, by archaeological searches, in inscriptions incised in stone, is associated with an interest in geometrical proportion. Various theories for the geometrical construction of the alphabet were developed, of which the earliest known (perhaps made in 1463) is in a manuscript in the Vatican executed by Felice Feliciano of Verona. A jubilant occasion in September 1464 when Felice Feliciano and others copied Roman inscriptions is referred to in the note to Plate 9. Other theories were put forward, notably by Moille, 1480; Pacioli, 1509; Dürer, 1525; Verini, 1526; and Tory, 1529. Tory goes farther, and, for example, relates the author's initials to the shape of a human head (quite unlike the author's).[1]

The swash capitals are seen in reticent association with formal roman capitals in Plate 59, whilst in Plate 69a they swing about as in a country dance.

Capitals were thought of as something different from minuscules and so upright capitals would be used with slanting minuscules and perhaps placed apart as in Plate 8. Arrighi firmly expressed a wish that capitals should always be drawn upright.

Formal and Cursive Script

In the appreciation of italic handwriting, and the attendant discrimination, it is important to see that some hands are formal and are almost or quite free of urgency, and will respond but little to hastening pressure, for there is something in the construction of the letters of these set scripts that requires more attention and precision and more pen-lifts than it is possible to give to a rapid script. One of the cursive principles is that speed tends to reduce or control the number of pen-lifts (though it does not follow that handwriting to be current should have no pen-lifts within words: i.e. every letter joined). Another feature to be noted is that in some italic scripts shown in this book, principally those of the writing manuals, the pen has not hurried because the script is a model or a standard from which one will depart inevitably as speed is developed. The model, as a starting-point for the learner, must show precise form and indicate intention. The best model will be that which is organized for speed but proceeds slowly: in a sense it is the horse that walks but can gallop fast enough. The hurtling movements of the pen following hard on the heels of thought are not adequately represented in this book, though Cellini's letter is an example. Raphael's sensitive and more controlled script also races across the page, with a rider's hand upon reins.

There is also, of course, the writing that is precise and executed at some pace, but which is not intended as a model. It may be seen in a letter of ceremony written with the distinction of the occasion, if not always displaying a calligrapher's technique. Grace has been much in mind as well as function. An interesting example is the letter of Pasqual Spinula (Plate 21), where a hand of notable quality, worthy of Arrighi, shows a casual attitude to the distribution of ink. One can mark when the writer dipped his pen into a too fluid ink.

[1] *A Book of Scripts*, by A. Fairbank, fig. 9.

There are then, formal scripts (e.g. the *cancellaresca formata* of Plate 42), set cursives (e.g. Arrighi's exemplars), and free cursives (Plate 13), and there are scripts which are not purely formal, set, or free.

Other classifications of nomenclature are that the formal bookhand related to the printer's roman letters (*littera antiqua*) is called humanistic, whilst the informal or cursive (italic) hand, is humanistic cursive. One of the italic hands of the fifteenth century was imitated in type and called by Aldus *cancelleresco italico*. Of the various humanistic cursives (*cancellaresca corsiva*) used for writing papal briefs, a standardized version written by Arrighi was called by him *littera cancellarescha* in his first manual and also *litera da brevi* in his second. Palatino held that *cancellaresca formata* had nothing about it that could be called *cancellaresca* and served only for the writing of small books. He comments on its rounded quality, its proportions, serifs, and pen-lifts. Shakespeare uses the term 'sweet Roman hand' and Ascham writes of Elizabeth's handwriting: 'Nothing can be more elegant than her handwriting whether in the Greek or Roman character.' Doubtless, both Shakespeare and Ascham refer to italic. Pierre Hamon, the Huguenot writing-master, refers to *lettre italique* and Jean de Beauchesne titles a model 'Italique hande'. One of the English medieval court hands is 'Chancery' and this is another reason why the author prefers to write of italic handwriting, and not of the Chancery hand.

Slope

The eye is very sensitive to the perpendicular. The vertical letter is poised and static. The sloping letter expresses movement and is dynamic. It is natural enough that a letter made formally, without urgency, should be vertical, and that the flying pen should suggest by the trail of its movements its progression from left to right.

Amphiareo's rather formal script is upright. The slope towards the right of the models of Arrighi, Tagliente, and Palatino, and also of the italic types of Aldus and Arrighi, is not more than 7 or 8 degrees from the perpendicular (one-twelfth of a right-angle): enough to make a perceptible slant but not such as to distort letters or to make them appear to be tumbling. Cresci, whose holding of the pen is different from that of Palatino, slants his letter twice as much. In some copperplate models the slant is more considerable, and in this connexion it is interesting to find Dickens writing of 'the rain slanting down like the lines they used to rule in the copy-books at school, to make the boys slope well'. The contemporary printer's italic types, since they are needed for purposes of contrast, have a greater slant than the best of the humanistic cursives and the types of Arrighi, and are accordingly less legible. In designing the type called Monotype Bembo Narrow italic, the author sloped the letters 5 degrees only.

Joins

Niccolò Niccoli, doubtless conversant with the diagonal join of some medieval script, borrowed it and incorporated it in his version of the Caroline minuscule, and thus produced a new cursive letter. The upstroke, made with an easy sideways movement, may form part of a letter as well as a join. It is an aid to currency unsuited to the making of circular or semicircular motions, and it is an expression of that force which caused the italic letter to be narrower than Roman. The humanistic cursives of the late fifteenth century, however (and this is but a guess), may have owed less to Niccoli's invention and more to inevitable changes when a formal hand is written quickly. In either case, the upstroke is significant.

Although it can be taken as a general rule that Renaissance italic alphabets are conditioned by the upstroke, it is necessary to remark that Edward Johnston and his pupils have written italic hands that were quite formal in respect of the construction of letters, words, and set-out, and were, indeed, narrowed Caroline, taking shape by compression and not because a sideways motion of the pen was a very good way of making an upstroke or a diagonal join and of saving time and effort. A change in a system of movements produces a different script.

Just how significant is the diagonal join to a cursive italic hand can be seen by a study of the models of Arrighi, Tagliente, and Mercator. For example, the two upstrokes in the letter *a* when the second has been extended into a join are certainly related.

For contemporary correspondence to be written with speed the diagonal join must be exploited as much as possible. The aim is to write without the contact of pen and paper being broken up too much. Pen-lifts give refreshment and allow adjustment of the hand as it passes across the paper. They occur frequently in the italic hand because certain letters do not readily run on to others. If, however, joins are not utilized as may be then a help is turned into the hindrance to speed we see in so many Elizabethan italic hands.

The diagonal join will be noted to serve legibility and appearance by its automatic control over the spacing of letters. The professional calligrapher spaces and places by his eye, but the diagonal join does as much as trained sight when it occurs.

The hairline upstroke generally rises at an angle of about 45 degrees to the writing line. In Plate 65b Tagliente shows two hands, the lower one being different from the upper one by reason of a difference in the angle of the hairline, which narrows and elongates the letter and blackens the inscription. The diagonal join looks less natural in the models of Lucas than in those of Arrighi.

Another form of join is the horizontal extension of the cross-strokes of *f* and *t*. In contemporary practice the letters *o*, *v*, and *w* have similar horizontal extensions which make convenient joins.

The practice of joining *c* and *t* and *s* and *t* by ligatures above the letters, which is charming but archaic and inexpedient, had begun some centuries prior to the Renaissance.

Ascenders and Descenders

Ascenders help identification and therefore legibility but present a difficulty in their formation when writing with speed. The clubbed ascender of the Caroline minuscule takes on a slightly more decorative form in fifteenth-century humanistic hands, but still with the emphasis of initial form generally on the left-hand side of the ascender. The italic serif when quickly executed might loop with a sharply turning movement to left or right or become a flourish or a hook. Another serif is that which might be called a barb. Arrighi, who was concerned to simplify the teaching of the *cancellarescha* hand, advises his readers that to gain unity in the script the ascenders of *b*, *d*, *h*, *k*, and *l*, should be equal in height and with the top made in the same way as an *a*. Both Arrighi and Palatino begin the *a* with a returning stroke, leading in from left to right and retracing its path. With the ascenders the top or head-piece is to be a little thicker than the line. If this means that the top is to be thicker than the stroke made naturally by the pen then the movement is in the nature of a narrow loop and obviously the parent of the bulbous tops of the letters in the models of Hercolani.

Arrighi holds that the descenders should be of equal length below the line and his *f*, *p*, *q*, *x*, and *y* terminate with a flattened left-ward curve. Arrighi's rule is not followed by some other papal scribes writing briefs at about the time of the publication of his books and this points to the standardization of his teaching.

An interesting study of ascenders and descenders is afforded by Plates 13 and 18. The ascenders in the 'Cheke hand' have been referred to on p. 31.

Grace and Pattern

The two prime and functional qualities of handwriting, namely legibility and expedience, are claimed for the italic hands of today. The early italic scripts also delight the sight and elevate artistic standards of penmanship, and it is for this reason this book is made. Their beauty is in many features which can be indicated, as well as the less obvious and individual expression of human character and personality. Grace abounds, in line and shape, in pattern and rhythm. Rhythmical pattern springs from forward movements and the sympathetic shaping of letters to accord with the motions. Harmony of style has been achieved by the courses of the pen, regularized, ordered, and integrated, and by spacing and placing. Handwriting is a 'musical' art.

Note for instance, in the model by Lucas shown in Plate 82, the clean and clear letter shapes and their exquisite proportions; the pen-character with its regular incidence of thicks and thins and gradations; the slight slope of the marching script; the pattern of the lines and the secondary patterning between them; and the unity resulting from these pleasing features and the harmonious spacing of letters, words, and lines. All these characteristics are made by controlled movements of the pen.

Movements of the pen in the act of writing are never at a consistent speed. Dodington certainly wrote the hand shown in Plate 47 more quickly than the one in Plate 46, and we appreciate that with speed movements occur which are more natural to the hand and less the product of control by eye and thought. His pointed script is not a slow version of the faster hand but a different hand. What relieves the pointed script from a possible though serene dullness is that there is a mixture of flattened curves (notable in both of his scripts and a common feature of italic) with the straight strokes.

In Raphael's hand (Plate 13) one feels a sense of delicacy of touch, of finger on the quill, and of the quill on the paper; and this is most evident when the pen lands from a pen-lift to form an ascender, or takes off at the termination of a descender.

A sheet of writing presents a pattern, more or less pleasing according to the shapes of letters and their arrangement. Primarily the pattern is made of a series of horizontal strips or bands, broken up by pen-lifts. The intervals between letters and words need be slight for the purposes of legibility: this is clearly demonstrated by a printed page. The quick and jerky movements of the hand across the sheet may share with the eye the measuring of the spacing of words, but taking more than a moiety of control. The spacing of letters too is not a matter decided by the sight only:

the general rhythm of the rapid hand and the character of the joins take much authority. The trained eye of the penman when writing with precision secures an appearance of equally spaced units building up the word, and the diagonal join co-operates (cf. Plates 11, 18, and 65b). Indeed the diagonal join is often more efficient at spacing than the eye.

A secondary patterning occurs by the extensions of letters: that is, from the ascenders and descenders which invade the white territory between the strips and perhaps from the contraction marks flourished above the words (cf. Plate 18). Some of the charm of the letters from Raphael and the Archbishop of Siena and the models of Amphiareo and Lucas certainly lies in the adequate spacing of the lines and the lively strokes which spring from the patterned bands and release the inscription from too great a discipline. A roman hand may have the lines closely spaced and the whole becomes a massed pattern, but italic writing, with its long ascenders and descenders, looks best when the lines are well apart. There is no virtue in letters fouling others.

Quills

A feature of Edward Johnston's teaching of formal penmanship was the insistence on sharpness of pen-stroke. This can be achieved by writing with a quill which has been cut to a sharp bevelled writing-edge. Such a pen in writing a roman hand is not pushed against its edge and is capable of making very fine hairlines. In writing a cursive hand the quill calls for a light touch. Arrighi and Palatino make it clear enough how to cut a quill, but one would like to know more of the final finesse of trimming the nib, and whether paring as well as wear, paper, or ink explained the lack of an acute contrast of thicks and thins in some of the scripts illustrated. In cutting a quill one can provide for stiffness or flexibility by the length of the slit, the shaping of the quill, and by the choice of a hard or soft quill. Today the easy-running metal pen, whether dip-pen or fountain-pen, is of service to italic writers.

The advice on choosing a quill given in *The Petie Schole* by Francis Clement (London, 1587) is: 'Of quills, the fayrest, whitest, and roundest are best, the third and fourth of the wing of goose, or raven: but where these are not, the pinnion quill hath no fellow.' Arrighi says the quill should be round, smooth, and hard and not too thick, whilst Hamon considers it should be long, clean, dry, and little laden with fat. Tagliente preferred the quill of the domestic goose to that of the wild goose.

Palatino held that it did not matter whether the quill was taken from the left or the right wing—the curvature from the left wing was then and still is generally regarded as more suitable to the right hand. The most satisfactory goose quills the author has used were those from Hudson Bay geese, but he preferred the swan quill for its larger size.

Ink

Recipes for making gall inks appear in sixteenth-century writing books. A version by Mr. H. R. Hughes of the recipe in Palatino's *Libro nel qual s'insegna a scrivere* is as follows:

'To Make Ink'

'Select for this three ounces of gallnuts that are small, heavy for their size, and wrinkled and pound them up roughly into not oversmall fragments. Then put them to soak in half a winejugful of wine, or of rainwater which is really rather the better, and leave them thus as an infusion in the sun for one or two days. Then take two ounces of copperas, or of Roman vitriol well coloured and finely ground, and stirring the said gallnuts solution with a fig stick put them into it and leave it thus in the sun for another day or two. Then, again stirring a little, put in an ounce of gum Arabic which should be translucent, glistening and well split-up, and leave it thus all day. And to make it lustrous and beautiful add a few pieces of pomegranate peel and bring it up to a simmer over a very slow fire. Then strain it and keep it in a glass or a well-stoppered lead container and it will be perfect.'

Mr. Hughes remarks that 'Roman vitriol is a crystalline sulphate of iron occurring native in the environs of Rome. Copperas is also sulphate of iron. The difference, though its causation would not have been known at the time Palatino wrote, consists of this: copperas is or should be ferrous sulphate; ferrous sulphate oxidizes on exposure to the ferric salt and one would expect supplies of the natural variety to be contaminated at times, hence Palatino's injunction to check that it be well coloured: i.e. bright green and not muddy-looking.'

Half a winejugful of wine would equal one-quarter of a full-sized bottle of Chianti.

The proportions of the constituents differ slightly in the recipes in Beauchesne's *A Booke Containing Divers Sortes of Hands* and Francis Clement's *The Petie Schole*.

Included in 'Rules made by E.B. for his Children to learne to write bye' in Beauchesne's book are the following:

'To Make Common Yncke'

To make common yncke of vvyne take a quarte,
Two ounces of gomme, let that be a parte,
Fyue ounces of Galles of copres take three,
Longe standing dooth make it better to be:
Yf wyne ye do want, rayne water is best,
And asmuch stuffe as aboue at the least:
Yf yncke be to thicke, put vinegre in:
For water dooth make the colour more dymme.

'To Make Special Black Yncke'

Yf that common yncke be not to your minde,
Some lampblacke thereto with gome water grinde:
Each paynter can tell, howe yt shoulde be done,
The cleaner out of your penne it will roone:
The same to be put in horne or in leade,
No cotton at all, when longe yt hath stayde,
The bottom will thicke, put more common yncke.
And it will be good well sturred, as I thinke.

Clement's proportions are the same as those of Beauchesne. He adds the advice that: 'To boyle the sayd stuffe together a little upon the fire would make it more speedy for your writyng: but the unboyled yeldeth a fayrer glosse, and longer indureth.'[1] It will be noted that Beauchesne was not averse to diluting his special ink (i.e. a carbon ink) with his gall ink.

Miss M. Thérèse Fisher in *A Calligrapher's Handbook* (book containing much valuable information about inks, pigments, pens, vellum, and the art of gilding) quotes an Italian proverb:

'Una due tre e trenta
A far la bona tenta.'

as giving the proportions of one part gum, two parts of vitriol, three of gall, in 30 of water.

Gall inks tend to fade to brown tints and sometimes have eaten through paper,

[1] Cf. *A Book of Scripts*, p. 15.

which has made selection of antique examples for reproduction difficult. The inks used by professional scribes writing bookhands that have retained their blackness are carbon inks (i.e. inks made of lamp-black produced by burning oil, &c.). Today a scribe would probably rub down a stick of Chinese ink in a little water, adding perhaps a drop of gum water, but carbon inks can be purchased in liquid form.

Italic Types

The first use of an italic type was by Aldus Manutius in 1501. The type was obviously based on an existing italic hand, but certainly not on the writing of Petrarch, as used to be said. It was cut by Francesco Griffo of Bologna. This italic, though small and having numerous ligatured letters, has sufficient clarity to be read continuously, but its success was due also to its economy: classics were printed in volumes of pocket-book size. The Aldine italic was popular and copied by other printers but eventually gave way to the types of Arrighi: i.e. economy came to count less than augmented clarity and aesthetic appearance.

Arrighi's first type, a superb italic, was used only in his writing-book *Il Modo de temperare le penne* and resembles his cancellaresca model. The second type was first used in 1524 when he returned to Rome from Venice and worked as a printer of small books of calligraphical style in association with Lautitius Perusinus, who was probably an engraver of seals. To this type were added two Greek letters to conform to the theories of spelling of Gian Giorgio Trissino. Plate 63 shows a later use of this charming type. A third type, this time with bracketed serifs to ascenders, was added to Arrighi's equipment in 1525. A copy of it cut in 1923 from the type of a book printed in 1539 by Antonio Blado, viz. *Vita Sfortiae* by Paolo Giovo, became the first of the so-called Chancery types of today: and is known as Monotype Blado. Mr. Stanley Morison chose this type for association with Monotype Poliphilus Roman, and it has been much admired. In addition to Blado's a very fine version of Arrighi's third type was used in the sixteenth century by the Parisian printer, Simon de Colines.

Arrighi's capitals were upright, whether roman or swash and whether in type or writing.

The penman may learn from Arrighi's types as the printer may learn from his scripts.

A very lively type is in use in Tagliente's manual but as a type it is rather too calligraphical in style and it has a slope twice as great as the types of Arrighi.

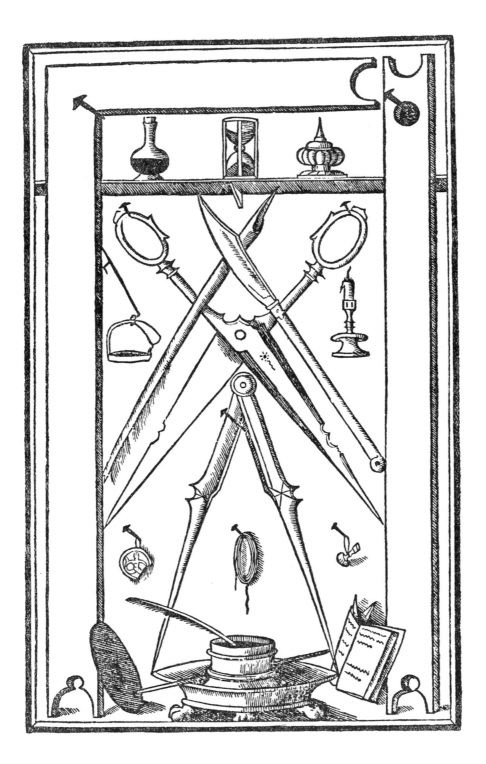

NOTES
by Berthold Wolpe

NOTES TO PLATES

I

ALCUIN'S BIBLE. Caroline minuscule.

France, ninth century. British Museum. Add. MS. 10546. In Latin. Vellum, 449 leaves. 19¾ × 15 inches.

Biblia Sacra Latina, ex versione vulgata. Written in double columns consisting of 50 lines each, in black ink with vermilion rubrication. The book of Psalms, however, has 52 lines. Length of line 4⅝ inches. Blind ruling impressed with a sharp stylus. Although this hand is often credited to the reform instituted by Alcuin, more recent opinion points to earlier origins, e.g. Maurdramnus Bible written at Corby in 750 described by Dr. E. A. Lowe.[1] It should be noted that the letter *n* is written without a pen-lift—a cursive characteristic.

Alcuin or Alchinus was born in Yorkshire in *c.* 735. In 796 he was nominated by Charlemagne Abbot of St. Martin at Tours. Here he founded a school and scriptorium which became centres of study and reform. According to a letter of Alcuin of the year 799 to Gisla, sister of the Emperor Charlemagne, he was then still deeply occupied in the emendation of the Old and New Testaments. The next year Charlemagne received from Alcuin the completed manuscript of the Bible.

Even if the style of lettering known as Caroline Minuscule may not have been formulated at Tours, the pre-eminence of Tours as a centre of learning has helped to spread its use and Alcuin's connexion with the Emperor must have given it additional importance as an authoritative style of lettering.

Folio 249 r. of this manuscript is written in an earlier hand which was superseded by the Caroline script employed for the rest of the manuscript.

2*a, b*

CICERO: DE ORATORE. Writing by Poggio.

Italy, 1428. Florence Bibl. Laur. Plut. 50.31. In Latin.

Poggio Bracciolini (1380–1459) was the first of the humanists to write a formal bookhand in the style which later in the century served as a pattern for the roman

[1] E. A. Lowe, *Codices Latini Antiquiores*, Part VI, O.U.P., 1954.

type. This is the true *lettera antiqua formata* based upon the Caroline hand. Not only do the letters of the text follow the earlier tradition but the illuminated initial is based upon the Italian romanesque white vine decoration. An interesting contrast is afforded by the juxtaposition of the opening and closing pages of the book: initial with early white vine decoration and colophon with fine and well-spaced capitals. The popularity of this text amongst the humanists is shown by the fact that it was one of the first books of the Subiaco Press (Sweynheim and Pannartz, 1465).

2*c*

AMMIANUS MARCELLINUS. Writing by Niccolò Niccoli.

Italy, Florence Bibl. Naz., Marc. I. v. 43. In Latin.

The advent of humanistic revival brought with it a great and urgent demand for classic texts. The few that survived the ravages of the dark ages, mostly written in Carolingian or post-Carolingian hands, were copied with all the necessary speed if they could not be bought.[1] This speed is a most important factor in the growth of the italic out of the roman or to use the expressions of Niccolò Niccoli's time: *lettera anticha corsiva* out of *lettera anticha formata*.

On the other hand one may say that the scholars who were used to the late medieval cursive as an epistolary, every-day hand, employed its characteristic diagonal upstrokes in their cursive which was also speedily written, but simplified in form and thus purer and more legible in style than the medieval scripts.

3

LETTERS OF PLINY THE YOUNGER. Anonymous scribe.

Italy, 1455. British Museum. Add. MS. 12007. In Latin. Paper, 98 leaves. $10\frac{1}{8} \times 8\frac{1}{4}$ inches.

Written in pale brown ink in an informal *anticha corsiva* with rubrication in sanguine. The manuscript has exceptionally wide margins. The last page was chosen to show the dated colophon, in stately capitals, which are in lively contrast to the small fluent patterning of the minuscules.

[1] According to Vespasiano da Bisticci, Niccoli once bought in Lubeck with the help of Cosimo de' Medici for the sum of 100 ducats a 'Pliny the Younger' of which no copy could be found in Italy at that time.

4

A FUNERAL ORATION BY PETRO MARCELLI. Writing by Marcus de Cribellariis (Mark of Vicenza).

Italy, 1478. British Museum. Add. MS. 19061. In Latin. Vellum, 20 leaves. 7⅜×4⅜ inches.

'Petri Marcelli pro ill°. P. Andrea Vendramino (Duce Venetorum) funebris oratio.' This oration is the first item in a codex containing six different books, some of them partly written on paper and all in a fluent upright italic with tied letters.

The first page has a decorated initial and an illumination with the arms of the Doge Vendramini.

The text is written by Mark of Vicenza in black ink with delicate ruling in brown. The last page carries the scribe's colophon:

MARCUS VICENTINUS SCRIPSIT. CALA/MO VOLANTI

Andrea Vendramini died in 1478. The full name of the scribe is Marcus de Cribellariis. According to the information given by James Wardrop to Sir Sydney Cockerell[1] there are two manuscripts in the Biblioteca Bertoliana at Vicenza, which were completed in August and October 1481, that are signed Marcus de Cribellariis Civis Vicentiae. After the date in the first of these (a Horace) are the words *Venetis scripsit*. We therefore take it that the manuscript from which we reproduce a page was also written in Venice. The roman hand of Mark of Vicenza is shown on plate xx of *Writing & Illuminating, & Lettering* by Edward Johnston.

5

ONOSANDER: DE OPTIMO IMPERATORE. Writing by Hippolytus of Luna.

Italy, 1494. Harvard College Library. MS. 179H. In Latin. Vellum, 174 leaves. 8½×5¾ inches.

Manuscript signed by the scribe: 'Hippolyti Lunensis manu.' Hippolytus was not only famous as a scribe, but also as an illuminator.

According to the opening inscription this book was intended for King Alphonso of Aragon, King of Naples, but is not mentioned in De Marinis' *La Biblioteca Napoletana dei Re d'Aragona*, as being included in the King's library. The text page shows a clear letter which holds its own against the rich formal border. The writing is

---

[1] *Book Handbook* 1952, vol. i, No. 2.

almost upright and shows very little contrast of thicks and thins. The white vine border, which earlier in the century was a mere copy of the romanesque model, has now been considerably enlivened and displays here a greater intricacy and brilliance of design.

This scribe is represented at the British Museum by four manuscripts, namely: Harl. 3481, Harl. 3482, Add. MS. 15273, and Add. MS. 15654. We find in William Morris's Notebook that Harl. 3481 was one of the manuscripts which he consulted at the British Museum.

6

PETRUS CARMELIANUS: LAUS ANGLIÆ. Writing by the author.

England, 1486. British Museum. Add. MS. 33736, 3 (Grenville). In Latin. Vellum, 11 leaves. 7½ × 5¼ inches.

'Petri Carmeliani Brixiensis poetæ suasoria Læticiæ ad Angliam pro sublatis bellis ciuilibus et Arthuro principe nato epistola.'

A Latin poem composed and probably written by Petrus Carmelianus in praise of England and of her King, Henry VII. Dedicated to him in 1486 on the occasion of the birth of Prince Arthur. In the same year the King granted the poet a pension.

The manuscript has illuminations with the royal arms of England supported by angels, and a border of white and red roses, a white hound and the Tudor dragon.

The writing of this and of Plate 7 are shown as sloped romans with a tendency towards italic.

A similar manuscript was dedicated by Carmelianus four years earlier to Edward, Prince of Wales (afterwards Edward V) and is also preserved in the British Museum (Royal MS. 12 A. XIX).

7

PETRARCH: EPISTLES. Anonymous scribe.

Italy, 1497. British Museum. Add. MS. 22555. In Latin. Vellum, 203 leaves. 11 × 7⅞ inches.

'Francisci Petrarchae Epistolarum de rebus familiaribus Libri Octo.' Prefixed is an epistle 'de administratione regni'.

'Fran. Pet. Thomae Messanesi. S.P.D. Addubitationis de Thyleinsula rescriptio: varieque ibi de ea insula opiniones', Book 3, letter I.

Written in a sturdy sloping bookhand without any diagonal joins. With illuminated initials and a decorative border on fol. 1 which contains the arms of Acquaviva, surmounted by a coronet.

The book is an exact copy of Manilio's edition of Petrarch, Venice, 1492. This illustrates the fact that at this time a hand-written book was still preferred by some to a printed edition.

Petrarch's letter about Ultima Thule, of which we reproduce a page, is of special interest to the English reader as it contains a reference to Richard de Bury (1281–1345), the father of the English Protorenaissance and the author of that famous treatise on the love of books, *Philobiblon.*

In 1330 and 1333 de Bury, who was chancellor to the King, visited Avignon and probably on the second mission met the great Petrarch, who asked de Bury's opinion as to where Ultima Thule was situated. De Bury evasively replied that he would refer to his books on his return to England; but even Petrarch's further inquiries remained unanswered.

In this letter Petrarch also gives the following laudatory description of Richard de Bury:

'. . . Viro ardentis ingenii, nec letterarum inscio, et qui ut in Britania genitus: atque educatus: abditarumque rerum ab adolescentia supra fidem curiosus talibus praesertim questiunculis enodandis aptissimus videretur.'

'. . . a man of ardent genius and of no little learning, born and schooled in Britain and incredibly devoted, from youth onward, to the study of out-of-the-way matters; and particularly adept at unravelling such vexing little problems.'

It is significant that King Edward III,[1] whose tutor Richard de Bury was, is the first of a line of kings who were able to write.

8

EUSEBIUS: CHRONICA. Writing by Bartolomeo Sanvito.

Italy, *c.* 1474. British Museum. Royal MS. 14 C. III. In Latin. Vellum, 150 leaves. 13⅛×9⅛ inches.

For other books by same hand, see also Plate 9 from B.M. MS. Stowe 1016 to which we venture to add B.M. MS. King's 24, Add. MS. 6051, Add. MS. 20927, and Harl. 2528.

Chronicle of Eusebius in the Latin version of St. Jerome. Written by the Paduan scribe and scholar Bartolomeo Sanvito of Padua, probably for Bernardo Bembo

[1] Cf. V. H. Galbraith, 'The Literacy of the Medieval English Kings', in *Proceedings of the British Academy,* 1935.

(father of the celebrated Cardinal Pietro Bembo) on the occasion of one or other of his embassies to Florence (1474–6 and 1478).

Sanvito wrote a very individual and elegant hand; one of his characteristic letter forms is the lower-case letter τ. The capitals are beautifully written and with use of many colours of delicate tones.

Fol. 17 contains an appeal, in gold capitals, to future copyists to collate their transcripts carefully.

9

INSCRIPTIONES ANTIQUÆ. Writing by Bartolomeo Sanvito.

Italy, 1500. British Museum. Stowe MS. 1016. In Latin. Vellum, 271 leaves. 10 × 6⅓ inches.

A collection of ancient inscriptions, mainly Latin but including a few in Greek. The author, Johannes Jucundus of Verona (1432/3–1515), was an architect and antiquary, who dedicated his book to Lorenzo de' Medici. Giocondo edited letters of Pliny and Vitruvius in 1514 and acted together with Raphael as adviser in the rebuilding of St. Peter's at Rome.

The place-names in this manuscript are in red, most of the inscriptions are in black, but a few are in gold, purple, blue, and green.

The book was written by Sanvito many years later than the one illustrated in Plate 8. The minuscules have not changed but are now shakily written, and much more so than the capitals.

His lines of capitals combine the fluency of script with the noble spacing of the Augustan inscriptions. The large inscriptional initial letter E is in gold in the original manuscript.

The Renaissance is notable for its interest in classical texts and inscriptions. As the author was an important member of the society of Paduan and Veronese humanists, that famous account comes to mind of an excursion of their members to the Lake of Garda in search of ancient monuments and inscriptions in September 1464. It is contained in additions made by Felice Feliciano to Francesco Scalamonte's *Life of Cyriacus of Ancona* (manuscript at the Biblioteca Capitulare in Treviso). According to Feliciano's jubilant narrative, the band of enthusiastic epigraphists, crowned with ivy and myrtle, after visiting the ruined temple of Diana, having made copies there of ancient inscriptions, sailed (accompanied by cyther play) across the lake in boats adorned with laurel, to give thanks in the temple of the Madonna for a happy and fruitful day. The result of this excursion was twenty-two inscriptions. We wonder whether Jucundus took part in this joyful venture.

IO

VINCIGUERRA: DE PRINCIPE LIBELLUS.

Italy, 1501–2. Victoria and Albert Museum. MS. L. 2320/1947. In Latin. Vellum, 18 leaves. 9 × 5⅜ inches.

This book is written by an unknown scribe to celebrate Leonardo Loredano's appointment to the office of Doge of Venice. The first page has a panel in blue with golden capitals: ANTONII | VINCIGUERRAE CHRO|NICI DE PRINCIPEL IBELLVS. Initial letter: gold on sanguine, and coat of arms within laurel wreath.

Note the various styles of commencing the ascenders of *b d h l* made by the scribe on the impulse of the moment. The diagonal join gives the script a sense of movement. This fast hand has some affinity with the script of Arrighi and of Tagliente.

There is a portrait painting of Loredano by Giovanni Bellini in the National Gallery, London, and one by his brother, Gentile Bellini, in the Carrara Academy, Bergamo.

II

HADRIANUS: DE ROMANAE ECCLESIAE POTESTATE. Anonymous scribe.

Italy, *c.* 1490. Harvard College Library. In Latin. 26 leaves. 11⅛ × 6 inches.

The page shown here is from an unrecorded work of Adriano Castellesi of Corneto (*c.* 1458–1521) who held office in Italy and England, including the bishoprics of Hereford, and of Bath and Wells.

The long ſ with descending vertical finial is an archaic form which later in the sixteenth century developed into a curved ending (cf. Arrighi's examples).

The late James Wardrop was of the opinion that this incomplete manuscript had affinities of the utmost interest with the semi-formal hand shown in Edward Johnston's book *Writing & Illuminating, & Lettering*. (See James Wardrop in *Harvard Library Bulletin*, vol. vii, No. 2.)

12

A LETTER WRITTEN BY BARTHOLOMAEUS CHALCUS.

Italy, 1498. British Museum. Egerton MS. 2016. In Italian. Paper. 11⅜×8 inches.

Bartholomaeus Chalcus (secretary to the Duke of Milan) to the Duke; Milan, 16 June 1498.

A letter on unruled paper written in great haste with frequent dipping of pen. Certain letters are very round, but the terminals of the descenders angular.

The same volume at the British Museum contains a letter by Tristanus Chalcus to Bartholomaeus Chalcus dated 19 March 1492.

13

A LETTER WRITTEN BY RAPHAEL.

Italy, 1508. Vatican Library. In Italian. Paper. 10½×8 inches.

A letter by Raphael da Urbino to Simone de Baristo di Carla da Urbino written from Florence on 11 or 21 April 1508, shortly before he was summoned to Rome by Pope Julius II.

A puzzling circumstance is that he was nominated on 4 October 1509 a scriptor of apostolic briefs by Julius II who made him soon afterwards painter to his palace (‘*che assegna a lui, "pittore nel suo palazzo", quel'ufficio, vacante per la morte di Vincenzo Capucci, e con esso gli onori, oneri ed emolumenti relativi.*’ A. Venturi, *Storia dell'arte italiana*, vol. ix, part 11, p. 17).

This letter is written with speed and sensitivity and is yet very precise and consistent in the repetition of letter forms. There is a careful nineteenth-century facsimile engraving of this document.

14

A LETTER FROM PETRUS CARMELIANUS.

England, 1496. British Museum. Egerton MS. 616. 5. In Latin. Paper. 13¾×12 inches.

Letter from Petrus Carmelianus, of Brescia (? 1460–1527), then Latin Secretary of Henry VII, to Ferdinand and Isabella of Spain, dated London, 2 July 1496.

It is intriguing to compare this developed italic of the King's diplomatic secretary with that of the court poet's bookhand shown in Plate 6, written ten years earlier.

15

A LETTER FROM HENRY VIII. Writing by Andreas Ammonius.

England, 1515. British Museum. Cotton MS. Vitellius B. II, f. 180. In Latin. Paper. 8 × 11¼ inches.

A complimental letter from Henry VIII to the Marquis of Mantua, dated: Greenwich, 24 June 1515. The writer, Andrea Ammonio (1477–1517), was Latin Secretary to Henry VIII and a friend of Erasmus. He was born at Lucca and educated at Rome. Ammonius died in London of the sweating sickness.

16, 17

PAPAL BRIEFS TO CARDINAL WOLSEY. Writing attributed to Ludovico Arrighi.

(16) Italy, 27 August 1519. Public Record Office, London, S.P. 1. 19, f. 11. In Latin. Vellum. 5 × 18 inches.

(17) Italy, 15 October 1520. Public Record Office, London, S.P. 1. 21, f. 106. In Latin. Vellum. 5 × 17 inches.

Desires credence for the letters of Silvester, Bishop of Worcester.
  Signed: Ja. Sadoletus

Recommends to him Peter Corso, a Florentine merchant, trading at London. He is connected with the Pope's family.
  Signed: Ja. Sadoletus

Arrighi was *Scrittore de brevi apostolici*, as he proudly describes himself in *La Operina*. This fact has been known, of course, but no briefs of his hand had been identified till now. In the opinion of the authors these two were written by Arrighi.

18

A LETTER FROM THE ARCHBISHOP OF SIENA TO HENRY VIII.

Italy, 1517. British Museum. Cotton MS. Vitellius B. III, f. 196. In Latin. Paper. 10¾ × 7½ inches.

Letter from Giovanni Piccolomini (1475–1537), Archbishop of Siena and nephew of Pius III, to inform Henry VIII of his admission to the College of Cardinals, and to give an assurance of his loyalty, written on the very day of his elevation by Leo X. Rome, 3 July 1517.

The writing, presumably by Piccolomini's secretary, is notable for its qualities of sound construction, fluency, and grace.

Another letter (unsigned) with similar content and written on the same day, is in the Public Record Office (S.P. 1/15), but though addressed to Wolsey was intended for the Colonna family.

19

THOMAS LINACRE. Dedication of a book to Wolsey.

England, 1517. British Museum Library. In Latin. Vellum. $10\frac{3}{8} \times 8\frac{1}{4}$ inches.

Thomas Linacre was born at Canterbury in 1460. He was one of the Greek teachers of Erasmus of Rotterdam. For his studies in Italy see Introduction p. 30.

Linacre was a physician of Henry VIII and in 1517 brought out a Latin edition of Galen's *Preservation of Health* which he translated from the original Greek. The book, printed by Guillaume Rubé in Paris, was dedicated to Henry VIII. The dedication page reproduced here is written by Linacre on the back of the title-page of a copy of this work printed on vellum which he gave to Wolsey. A presentation copy on paper to Richard Fox, Bishop of Winchester, also with a fine dedication page in Linacre's hand, is preserved in the Library of the Royal College of Physicians. There is a small letter in humanistic cursive by Linacre in the British Museum addressed to the Florentine bookseller Pietro Machiavelli about the transcription of some books (Add. MS. 12107 f. 10).

20

A LETTER FROM J. M. GIBERTO TO CARDINAL WOLSEY.

Italy, 1524. Public Record Office, London, S.P. 1.—32–219. In Latin. Paper. $11\frac{1}{2} \times 7\frac{3}{8}$ inches.

The Calendar of State papers gives the following synopsis:

'J. M. Giberto to Wolsey:

There is no need to tell him the reasons why the Pope sent him to the French King and the leaders of the Imperial army, and that none of his propositions were listened to, as he will have heard all this from Melchior Langue. Was careful of the King's interest, not only in consequence of the Pope's orders, but from his remembrance of

Wolsey's kindnesses. Was pleased to see that the combatants, though disagreeing in everything else, agreed in their opinion of the valour and prudence of the King and Wolsey. Though this mission is fruitless, the Pope is satisfied with having shown to everyone that he has left nothing undone to secure peace. Acknowledges Wolsey's thanks for the services he has done him. Rome, 12 December 1524.'

Signed: 'Jo. Mattheus El. Veron.'

21

A LETTER FROM PASQUAL SPINULA TO CARDINAL WOLSEY.

England, 1528. Public Record Office, London. S.P. 1.—49-204. In Latin. Paper. 12½ × 8⅝ inches.

A part of a letter from Pasqual Spinula to Cardinal Wolsey written in London on 6 August 1528, concerning a cargo of alum which had been sequestrated. Spinula had been unwilling to wait on Wolsey during the prevalence of the sweating sickness.

This matter of the sequestrated alum had caused much diplomatic activity and among documents on the subject, either at the Public Record Office or the British Museum, are two papal briefs from Clement VII, two letters from Francis I and one from Louisa of Savoy; and six of the documents are written in fine italic hands. A pardon was granted in December 1530 to Balthazar, Pasqual, and Jeremy Spynnell, merchants of Genoa, for evading payment of customs on 2,000 quintals of alum imported into England and landed at the port of London. The name of the merchants is variously spelt: Spinula, Spinolle, Spinuli, Spinulis, Spinol, and Spynnell.

The upper part of the letter is reproduced in *A Handwriting Manual*. Another letter in the same superb hand is in the British Museum (Cotton MS. Vit. B. X). The ink appears to have been very liquid and to have run out of the pen quickly.

22

PART OF A LETTER FROM HENRY VIII.

England, 1530. Public Record Office, London. S.P. 1.—58-120. In Latin. Paper. 12¼ × 8 inches.

Opening page of a letter of Henry VIII to Ghinucci, Benet, and Casale, in the hand of a secretary. Dated 7 October 1530, Hampton Court and signed by the King at the head of the letter. The signature shows his characteristic black letter style with a final knot. The letter begins by saying that the King has received their joint and several letters dated Rome, 17 September, showing that their efforts with the Pope on the King's behalf had been fruitless.

23

A PAGE OF *VERSES AND DITIES MADE AT THE CORONATION OF QUEEN ANNE* BY JOHN LELAND AND NICHOLAS UDALL.

England, 1533. British Museum. Royal MS. 18. A. LXIV. In Latin. Paper, 16 leaves. $10\frac{5}{8} \times 7\frac{1}{2}$ inches.

A page from 'A copie of Diuers and sundry verses as well in Latin as in Englishe deuised and made partly by Jhon Leland and partely by Nicholas Vuedale' (Leland's are all Latin) on the occasion of the coronation of Queen Anne Boleyn at the pageants exhibited by the Mayor and Citizens of London on Whitsun Eve, 25 Henry VIII (31 May 1533). The poets of these verses and ditties, as they are called on a vellum slip pasted on fol. 1, were John Leland the antiquary (d. 1552) and Nicholas Udall al. Uvedale, the dramatist (Headmaster of Eton College, 1534–41, and of Westminster School, 1554–6). Both Leland's and Udall's verses are autograph.

That Leland who wrote so elegant an italic hand himself was appreciative of Roger Ascham's penmanship is shown in the following epigram:

Ad Rogerum Aschamum

Aschame, litterulas tam belle pingis, ut ipsa
    Graecia te scribam pervelit esse suum:
Ut velit esse suum, rerum caput, inclyta Roma,
    Quamvis Italicos scribere docta modos.
Sed calamos cur certo tuos attollere vates
    Carmine: sit virtus quum tua nota satis.

A further passage that shows Leland's practical interest in the teaching of italic handwriting, I noticed in the 1586 edition of Holinshed's Chronicle: 'He [Henry Fitzroy, Duke of Richmond] loued *John Leland* the reuerend antiquarie, who presented unto the said duke a booke of copies whereby he might learne to write Romane letters great & small as appeareth by this hexastichon, which I find amongst the said *John Leland*'s written epigrams in this manner set downe:

Quo Romano modo maiuscula littera pingi,
    Pingi quo possit littera parva modo,

Hic liber ecce tibi signis monstrabit apertis,
Princeps Aonii spes et alumne gregis;
Qui tibi si placeat (quod certe spero futurum)
Maxima pro parvo munere dona dabis.'

24

A LETTER WRITTEN BY HENRY FITZROY, DUKE OF RICHMOND, AT THE AGE OF SEVEN.

England, 1526. British Museum. Cotton MS. Vespasian F. III, f. 44. In English. Paper. $8\frac{5}{8} \times 7\frac{3}{8}$ inches.

A letter from Sheriff Hutton, dated 4 March, written by the young Duke to Wolsey, the Cardinal Legate.

'Please it your grace to be advertised that at this time I do write unto the same not only to make a demonstration of this my proceeding in writing . . . .'

The writing is an italic of even measure and the first used by a Tudor.

Henry Fitzroy (1519–36) was a natural son of Henry VIII and Elizabeth Blount (afterwards Talboys). It seemed that he was being groomed as the King's successor to the dismay of Catherine of Aragon. At the age of six he was made Duke of Richmond, a title Henry VIII himself had borne. In 1527 Richard Croke, who then was his tutor, said of him in a letter, that 'though only 8 years old he can translate any passage of Caesar'. Our comparison of master's and pupil's hands shows a definite influence of Croke on this gifted boy's writing at that time. In the same letter (P.R.O. S.P. 1/42) Croke complains that George Cotton, the Duke's gentleman usher and later his governor, tried persistently and perversely to teach the Duke and his schoolfellows to write the Secretary and to give up the Roman hand which Croke had taught the young Henry so well.

Croke implies that Cotton's incompetence to teach even that hand, Wolsey may judge from Cotton's autograph:

'Nec haec satis nocuisse contentus, animari pueros ut (quam a me dedicere scribere) *Rhomanam* contemnant et in meum contemptum dediscant. Sed neque hic diligentiae fucus maliciae deest. Nam ipse *secretariam* ipsos docet qualem autem ex ipsius autographo licet judicare.'

Croke after some further complaints denounces the artful Cotton for getting hold of the Prince's autographs and bartering them with some neighbouring abbots for hawks or trifles of that kind, to the detriment of the Prince's dignity.

'Deinde, quia hoc colore volent ad quoslibet in Cotoni commodum aut favorem principis autographae, et ignaris consiliariis et me invito puta ad abbates pro accipitribus et id genus nugis, contra quod tua Celsitudo jusserat, prostituta principis dignitate.'

For Leland's association with the Duke of Richmond see the note to Plate 23.

25

A PAGE OF A BOOK IN THE HANDWRITING OF PRINCE EDWARD (Edward VI).

England, 1546. British Museum. Harleian MS. 5087, f. 2. In Latin. Paper. $11\frac{1}{2} \times 7\frac{1}{4}$ inches.

A copy of a letter of Edward VI (1537–53) as Prince, in his own hand, to his tutor Dr. Richard Cox. 'In this the Prince playfully begs his almoner to take as much pleasure in his letters as others did in hunting and hawking: for letters were better than treasures. He then begs him to greet the King's secretary, sir William Paget, and to thank him for his present of a little sand-box' (from John Gough Nichol's *Literary Remains of Edward VI*).

The volume from which this letter has been reproduced contains forty-three of Edward's letters on eighteen leaves followed by some blank pages and then a number of his Latin exercises.

To quote from Edward's own manuscript journal or 'Chronicle' as he entitles it: 'At the sixth year of his age he was brought up in learning by Mr Doctor Coxe, who was after(wards) his almoner, and John Cheke, master of arts, two well learned men, who sought to bring him up in learning of tongues, of the scriptures, of philosophie, and all liberal sciences. Also John Belmaine, Frenchman, did teach him the French language' (transcribed from B.M. Cotton MS. Nero, Cx).

Edward's hand, whilst always clear and legible, is of rather formal stiffness; he never achieved the grace and distinction characteristic of his sister Elizabeth's and even of his brother the Duke of Richmond's style. That he took an interest in the shape of letters is shown in his note to Queen Katharine Parr, see our comments on Plate 29.

Bishop Latimer's conception of what a king's attitude to writing should be is made clear in one of seven sermons, preached by him before the young king in 1549.

Latimer said as an incentive to Edward's love of learning: 'He must be a student. He must write God's book himself . . . yet a king may take his pastime in hawking or hunting, or such like pleasures. But he must use them for recreation, ... He must write out a book himself. . . . And shall the king write it out himself? He meaneth he shall see it written, and, rather than he should be without it, write it himself.'

26

A PAGE OF *S. JOHANNI CHRYSOSTOMI HOMILIAE* BY JOHN CHEKE.

England, 1543. Library of St. John's College, Cambridge. MS. H. 18. In Latin. Paper, 43 leaves. 8 × 5½ inches.

A quarto manuscript on paper by Sir John Cheke (1514–57) dedicated to Henry VIII and traditionally attributed to his hand. Another manuscript given by him to King Henry is his Latin translation and commentary of *Plutarch on Superstition* at the Bodleian. This and a second copy at the British Museum may be in his writing.

Cheke was deeply interested in a new pronunciation of the classic languages and in a new system of writing English.

In my opinion his interest in these matters must have been stimulated, to say the least, by the books of Gian Giorgio Trissino, particularly by his *Epistola de le lettere nuovamente aggiunte ne la lingua Italiana*. On the page reproduced here we find the Greek letter omega, following Trissino's theory, used in the following lines: 1, 2, 10, 13, 14, and 15.

Cheke stood at the beginning of a line of English spelling reformers: Sir Thomas Smith, John Hart, and William Bullokar, to mention a few names of his century. In our own time Robert Bridges and Bernard Shaw tried to work on the same arduous task.

Strype comments on this side of Cheke's work: 'Another Piece of that exactness that was in Cheke, appeared in his Case about Orthography, that is for true and right Writing, as well as Pronouncing. And here both the Latin and our Mother Tongue fell under his correction. As for the Latin, that it might be spoken truly, and the syllables in Reading pronounced long or short, according to their Nature, he devised a Way to Write the Vowels according to their quantity. As the long Vowel O, after this manner like a Greek Omega, as in Uxωrem, liberωs.'

Cheke's influence can even be traced in a manuscript of Roger Ascham and in the letters of classically minded people such as Lady Jane Grey, see Plate 33, and William Bowyer, who sometimes used the omega in their own signatures.

27

A LETTER WRITTEN BY JOHN CHEKE.

England, 1549. British Museum. Lansdown MS. 2, f. 85. In English. Paper. 12 × 8⅜ inches.

A letter by Sir John Cheke to Anne, Duchess of Somerset, on his wife's behalf: she was then under her Grace's displeasure; dated 27 January 1549.

'Therefore he takes his pen and with words of the lowliest Submission makes his Application to her; not in the least excusing his Wife's Fault but only using Arguments proper to move and mollifie the Duchesses great Spirit.' Strype, *Life of Sir John Cheke*, 1705.

There is no knowing what caused the displeasure of the Duchess but it is fascinating to compare this letter with the facing plate: The application of 1549 is penned in haste and with great freedom, the Chrysostomus of 1543, however, is written slowly and deliberately.

A hundred years after the invention of printing the scholar was still capable of writing out slowly and carefully a book for his patron.

28

A LETTER WRITTEN BY PRINCESS ELIZABETH.

England, 1552. British Museum. Harleian MS. 6986, f. 23. In Latin. Paper. 12¼ × 8 inches.

Princess Elizabeth (1533–1603) to her brother King Edward VI in Latin dated from Ashridge, 20 September (probably 1552).

Address on outside: 'To the Kinges most Excellent Maiestie.'

She congratulates the King on his rapid and merciful recovery from a recent illness to which he fell a victim while he was in London. The letter also contains references to the opinions of Pindar and Homer on the transience of human life.

This document is almost a companion piece to the letter of Queen Katharine Parr reproduced on Plate 29. All through her life Queen Elizabeth maintained that same signature of proud elegance.

Roger Ascham is usually credited with teaching Princess Elizabeth her graceful style of writing. He certainly influenced it considerably. But it was beautiful even before Ascham's and his predecessor Grindal's tutorship began.

After careful comparison of several manuscripts I thought it seemed possible that it was Jean Belmain (see also note to Plate 25) who grounded her and her brother Edward in fine penmanship.

It was under Belmain's guidance that the young Princess translated, at the age of eleven, Margaret of Navarre's poem *Le Miroir de l'âme pécheresse*. This manuscript—her first literary work—which is now preserved at the Bodleian Library was offered by Elizabeth as a New Year's gift to Queen Katharine Parr whose own writing seems later to have served as a model to the young Princess. In the same year 1544 Belmain began to teach Prince Edward.

The earliest writing of Princess Elizabeth survives in a letter in Italian also addressed to Queen Katharine Parr dated 31 July 1544, beginning with the words: 'L'inimica fortuna invidiosa d'ogni bene . . .' (B.M. Cotton MS. Otho C. x, f. 235).

29

A LETTER WRITTEN BY KATHARINE PARR.

England, 1544. British Museum. Cotton MS. Vespasian F. III, f. 37. In Latin. Paper. $10\frac{1}{8} \times 7\frac{1}{8}$ inches.

Katharine Parr (1512–48) is known to have been gracious and kindly in her dealings with Mary, Elizabeth, and Edward, the children of Henry VIII. She married Henry, as his last wife, in 1543. In this letter Queen Katharine recommends the emended translation of Erasmus's work on the Gospel according to Saint John. The emendations were by Mallet. It is interesting to note the following two circumstances: that Francis Mallet (died 1570) was appointed chaplain to Princess Mary in 1544; and that Mary herself is known to have translated Erasmus's *Paraphrases of St. John*. The original Catalogue of the Cotton Library says: 'Queen Katharine (Parr) probably to Princess, afterwards Queen, Elizabeth, of whose handwriting this appears to be a copy' (Hanworth, 20 September, 1544) which is a curious statement considering not only the difference in age but also Elizabeth's style of writing at that time. In our opinion this letter is addressed to Princess Mary.

In a letter to Queen Katharine from Hunsdon, 10 June 1546 (MS. Harl. 5087, no. 9) Prince Edward pays compliments on her penmanship. He states that her last letter to him was written in the italic hand (*Romanis literis*) and so admirably that the Prince's preceptor could not be persuaded but that the Queen's secretary had written it, until he saw her signed name written equally well.

'*Etsi omnes literae tuae mihi dulces erant, tamen arridebant hae postremae literae prae ceteris, Regina nobilissima atque mater benevolentissima, ob quas ingentes tibi gratias ago. Sane vero in his video te diligentiam adhibuisse Romanis literis, ita ut non potuerit persuaderi preceptori meo quin Secretarius tuus scripserit, donec vidisset nomen tuum scriptum aeque bene.'*

A further letter of Edward to the Queen, this time in French, elaborates the same theme, praising her writing and inventiveness of letter forms, and expressing his reluctance to send her a sample of his less ingenious hand (B.M. Harl. MS. 6986).

'Je vous mercie, tresnoble et tresexcellente Roine, de voz lettres lesquelles vous m'envoiastes dernierement, non seulement pour la beaute de voz lettres, mais aussy pour l'invention des mesmes lettres. Car quand je voiois vostre belle escriture et l'excellence de vostre engin grandement precedant mon invention je nausois vous escrire. Mais quand je pensois que vostre nature estoit si bonne, que toute chose procedant d'un bon esprit et vouloir seroit acceptable, je vous ay escrit ceste lettre cy.

De ma maison de Hampton court.'

30

A TESTIMONIAL SIGNED BY SIX MEMBERS OF THE PRIVY COUNCIL.

England, 1550. British Museum. Lansdown 1236, f. 18. In Latin. Paper. 8 × 12⅝ inches.

A testimonial in favour of Vicentio Bellaci, a Florentine[1] who had served in the English Army, signed by six of the Privy Council. Four out of the six signatures are in italic:

E. Somerset—Edward Seymour, First Earl of Hertford and Duke of Somerset (1506—executed in 1552), the Protector, brother of Queen Jane Seymour.

W. Wilteshire—William Paulet (1485–1572), First Earl of Wiltshire (for one year only), and first Marquis of Winchester.

J. Warwyk—John Dudley (1502–53), Viscount Lisle, Earl of Warwick, Duke of Northumberland, father-in-law of Lady Jane Grey, executed in 1553 for resisting the succession of Mary to the throne.

J. Bedford—John Russell (1486–1555), First Earl of Bedford.

W. North—William Parr, Marquis of Northampton and Earl of Essex (1513–71), brother of Queen Katharine Parr.

H. Dorssett—Henry Grey, Third Marquis of Dorset, Duke of Suffolk, father of Jane Grey, created Duke in 1551, executed in 1554.

[1] Petruccio Ubaldini, also a Florentine, (cf. Plate 37) is said to have taken part in the campaign in Scotland in 1548. Another Italian also in the same campaign was a Captain Tiberio. Furthermore a company of Italian mercenaries under the command of one Malatesta helped to put down Ket's revolt in Norfolk in 1549.

It deserves mention here that an inventory dated 'the last of January 1550' of the household of the Earl of Warwick, who signed here in Secretary hand, contains a catalogue of his library. Among the forty books listed is one item of the utmost interest to us and never noticed before in this context, namely: *A boke to write the Roman hand.* This is the first time an italic copy-book is mentioned in English documents. The inventory, now at the Bodleian (Add. MS. c 94), was discovered in a lawyer's office in Oxford in 1874, neatly stitched together all round and hidden in the binding of a book.

31

A LETTER FROM THE KING OF POLAND.

Poland, 1555. Public Record Office, London. S.P. 69—6–72. In Latin. Paper. 10×9¼ inches.

Letter of Sigismund Augustus, King of Poland to Queen Mary. Written by a secretary in a well-formed slightly sloping italic. Most of the capital letters are very small, and only at the beginning of a new phrase do they range with the ascenders of the lowercase. The letter opens proudly with the King's name in well-spaced capitals and introduces Albert Criski, governor of Drobny, as Ambassador to her Majesty.

32

PART OF A LETTER FROM BARNABY FITZPATRICK TO EDWARD VI.

France, 1552. British Museum. Cotton MS. Caligula E. III, f. 273. In English. Paper. 9 inches tall.

Barnaby Fitzpatrick, the son and heir of Barnaby, Lord of Upper Ossory, was brought up with Prince Edward. He was the Prince's whipping boy, or, to put it more gently, his 'proxy for correction'. It is not reported whether this punishment was ever employed.

Barnaby was sent to the court of the King of France 'to learn fashions and manners, for the better serving of the King's majesty at his return' to quote from Edward's letter of introduction to the French King.

In another letter the King instructs his friend:

'First we would wish you, as much as you may conveniently, to be in the French king's presence, or at least in some part of his army where you shall perceive most business to be, and that for two causes: one is, because you may have more experience in the warrs, and see things that might stand you in stead another day; the other is, because you might be more profitable in the language; for our embassador, who may not weare harness, cannot well come to those places of danger, not seem so to serve the French king as you may, whom we sent thither for that purpose.'

The fast writing of Fitzpatrick here reproduced is from one of his letters in the Cotton collection, which reports to the King his experiences in the French campaigns. The document is damaged by fire, as are many in the Cotton collection.

33

PART OF A LETTER FROM LADY JANE GREY TO HENRY BULLINGER.

England, 1552. Zentralbibliothek, Zürich. R.P. 17 v. In Latin. Paper. 12 × 8 inches.

Second page of a letter from Lady Jane Grey (1537–54) to Henry Bullinger (1504–75), the Swiss reformer. This is from one of her three letters preserved at the Zentralbibliothek in Zürich.

Lady Jane was the daughter of Henry Grey, Duke of Suffolk—for his signature see Plate 30—and of Frances Brandon, Henry VIII's niece, so that through her mother she was in the royal succession. She was 'Jane the Queen' for nine days only and was executed in 1554 at the age of seventeen.

Her education was entrusted to John Aylmer (1521–94) who was in correspondence with the circle of Genevan reformers. One of them, John Ulmer, came to England through him and studied at Oxford at the Marquis of Dorset's expense; he granted Ulmer a yearly stipend of 30 crowns. The letter here reproduced was sent to Bullinger together with one by Ulmer of the same date.

To give an idea of the learned accomplishments of Lady Jane I can do no better than to quote Ascham's delightful reminiscence from his *Scholemaster*:

'Before I went into Germany, I came to Bradgate in Leicestershire, to take my leave of that noble lady Jane Grey, to whom I was exceeding much beholding. Her parents, the duke and duchess, with all the household, gentlemen and gentlewomen, were hunting in the park. I found her in her chamber, reading *Phaedo Platonis* in Greek, and that with as much delight as some gentlemen would read a merry tale in Boccace. After salutation, and duty done, with some other talk, I asked her, why she would leese such pastime in the park? Smiling she answered me; "I wist, all their sport in the park is but a shadow to that pleasure that I find in Plato. Alas! good folk, they never felt what true pleasure meant." "And how came you, madam," quoth I, "to this deep knowledge of pleasure? and what did chiefly allure you into it, seeing not many women, but very few men, have attained thereunto?" "I will tell you," quoth she, "and tell you a truth, which perchance ye will marvel at. One of the greatest benefits that ever God gave me, is, that he sent me so sharp and severe parents, and so gentle a schoolmaster. For when I am in presence either of father or mother; whether I speak, keep silence, sit, stand, or go, eat, drink, be merry, or sad, be sewing, playing, dancing, or doing anything else; I must do it, as it were, in such weight, measure, and number, even so perfectly, as God made the world; or else I am so sharply taunted, so cruelly threatened, yea presently sometimes with pinches, nips, and bobs, and other ways (which I will not name for the honour I bear them) so without measure misordered, that I think myself in hell, till time come that I must go to Mr. Elmer (Aylmer); who teacheth me so gently, so pleasantly, with such fair allurements to learning, that I think all the time nothing whiles I am with him. And when I am called from him, I fall on weeping, because whatsoever I do else but learning, is full of grief, trouble, fear, and whole misliking unto me. And thus my book hath been so much my pleasure, and bringeth daily to me more pleasure and more, that in respect of it, all other pleasures, in very deed, be but trifles and troubles unto me."

I remember this talk gladly, both because it is so worthy of memory, and because also it was the last talk that ever I had, and the last time that ever I saw that noble and worthy lady.'

This in fact shows a similar sentiment to that expressed by Prince Edward in his letter to Cox (see note to Plate 25). For a translation of Lady Jane's letter see *Original Letters relative to the English Reformation*, &c. Edited by Hastings Robinson, Parker Society, Cambridge, 1846.

34

TWO PAGES FROM A MANUSCRIPT BY ROGER ASCHAM.

England, 1542. Library of St. John's College, Cambridge. No. 360 L. 3. In Latin. Paper. $6\frac{5}{8} \times 4\frac{1}{2}$ inches.

'Expositiones quaedam Antiquae in Epistolam Diui Pauli ad Philemonem.'

A 12mo manuscript on paper composed and written by Roger Ascham as a New Year present to John Seton, also a Fellow of St. John's College, Cambridge. We reproduce here title-page and fol. 6.

As with John Cheke we are able to show Ascham's book and letter hand, in each case one of a number of varieties. Whilst Cheke's style of writing in the specimen shown indicates a certain nervous disposition, Ascham's remains in both more disciplined and polished. There are, however, letters of Ascham extant written in different and sometimes hurried styles.

35

A LETTER FROM PHILIP AND MARY. Writing attributed to Roger Ascham.

England, 1555. British Museum. Cotton MS. Vespasian F. III, Art. 47. In Latin. Paper. $7\frac{1}{8} \times 11$ inches.

Letter from Philip and Mary to Pope Marcellus II, recommending Nic. Hethe for the Archbishopric of York. Hampton Court. 4 May 1555.

Marcellus II (Marcello Cervini of Montepulciano) was Pope for a few days only, namely from 9 to 30 April 1555. The receipt of news of his death would explain why the letter was not dispatched.

The document is in the name of both King and Queen, but the seal is Mary's. The juxtaposition, character, and relative sizes of the royal signatures are significant.

The writing of this letter is attributed here to Roger Ascham. Ascham was Latin Secretary not only to Mary but also to Henry VIII and Edward VI. What Burckhardt has to say about the humanist scholar as secretary may be considered applicable here: 'There were two purposes, however, for which the humanist was as indispensable to the republics as to princes . . ., namely the official correspondence of the State, and the making of speeches on public and solemn occasions. Not only was the secretary required to be a competent Latinist, but conversely, only a humanist was credited with the knowledge and ability necessary for the post of secretary.' Roger Ascham must have excelled in these rare qualities, for Queen Mary found herself obliged to tolerate his nonconformity in religious matters.

36

A SPECIMEN BOOK WRITTEN BY BERNARDINO CATANEO.

Italy, 1545. Harvard College Library. MS. Typ. 246 H. In Italian. Vellum, 20 leaves. $5\frac{1}{2} \times 8$ inches.

This elegant calligraphic specimen book of twenty vellum leaves was written by Bernardino Cataneo of Siena for 'Signor Odoardo Ralyg, Gentiluomo Inglese'. Its contents are excerpts from Orlando Furioso and its date is 4 February 1545.

See article by James Wardrop, 'Six Italian Manuscripts in the Department of Graphic Arts', in *Harvard Library Bulletin*, vol. vii, 1953, p. 221.

37

A SPECIMEN BOOK WRITTEN BY PETRUCCIO UBALDINI.

England, 1550. British Museum. Royal MS. 14 A XVI, f. 17. In Italian. Paper. 7×11 inches.

Copy-book specimens of forty-eight styles of calligraphy by Petruccio Ubaldini, specially written for Edward VI and dated London, 20 July 1550. The examples are in Italian, French, and Latin. Some of the styles are named, e.g. *lettera mercantile* (fol. 15) and Napolitana (fol. 16). The initial letters of the forty-eight leaves form a sequence of two alphabets.

fol. 1 is signed: 'Di Londra il di xx di Iuglio 1550 Petruccio Vbal fiorno.'

fol. 42 has a centre panel with *Petrucchios Vbaldinus Florentinvs scribebat London, Anno DNI 1550 Edwardi vero regis regni quarto* flanked by two panels with microscopic writing.

38

A MADRIGAL WRITTEN BY MICHAEL ANGELO.

Italy. Library of the Uffizi, Florence. In Italian. Paper. $8\frac{1}{2}$×6 inches.

A madrigal of his own invention, 'Favours, though sweet, are annoying . . .', beautifully written by Michael Angelo Buonarotti (1475–1564).

From manuscript formerly at the Laurenziana, but now believed to be in the library of the Uffizi in Florence.

39

A LETTER TO MICHAEL ANGELO WRITTEN BY BENVENUTO CELLINI.

Italy, 1561. British Museum. Add. MS. 23139, f. 14. In Italian. Paper. $11\frac{1}{4}$×$8\frac{1}{2}$ inches.

A letter to Michael Angelo written by Benvenuto Cellini. Florence, 3 September 1561. Written swiftly in a free hand.

'Most excellent & most honourable Master Michelangelo.

Since I do not believe that any man born has been more appreciative of your worth than myself, of which I first became aware when I was working as a goldsmith and became enamoured of your unique powers, it seemed to me that I could only satisfy my honest ambitions by first coming somehow into contact with the wonderful art of sculpture and so always observing you with admiration, I gained a certain degree of honour which is entirely due to you.

Now considering that men in truth are obliged to love and to respect one another: I have a workman, whom I have taken as a companion because of his excellent qualities, and now for various reasons of his, he wishes to come to your beautiful city of Rome; he tells me that in the past he has done you service in making certain capitals for the great fabric of St. Peter's: since he is skilful in the art, I am most certain that they must have been satisfactory: & so I beg you, for love of me, to give him some work, for which I shall be most obliged to you: you know that I am always at your service: may God long preserve you in happiness. From Florence, 3 Sept. 1561.

always ready for your commands

Benvenuto Cellini'

40

GRIMANI'S *COMMENTARY ON ST. PAUL'S EPISTLE TO THE ROMANS.*

Italy, before 1538. Sir John Soane's Museum, London. In Latin. Vellum, 142 leaves. 13⅛×9¼ inches.

The manuscript is written in an upright italic with small capitals, very similar to an italic printing type of an unusual style used in Milan by the printer Castiglione in the 1540's (see *Fleuron*, vol. v, p. 100).

The initial word PAULVS in gold and beige, changing, with the fourth letter L in blue which gives a curious abrupt effect set against the harmonious border illumination. Elsewhere in the manuscript is a small tablet with gold lettering: MARINO GRIMA / NO.CAR / ET.LEGA / TO.PERV / SINO. PA / TRONO / SVO.JVLIVS / CROVATA / PINGEBA / T. This inscription is rubbed and difficult to read, therefore recorded here. In 1833 Sir John Soane bought the Grimani Commentaries and two other manuscripts from the Duke of Buckingham for £735.

Librum hunc, post eius primam scriptione, castigatiore reddimus is added on the last page in a personal italic hand.

Another manuscript illuminated by Clovio, and written by Sanvito, Horae B.M.V. Add. MS. 20927, is on show in the British Museum. Giulio Clovio, born in 1498 at Grizane in Croatia, was well famed as an illuminator and painter; his work is described in a monograph by J. W. Bradley.

41

CHURCH REGULATIONS. WRITING BY DE VITALIBUS.

Italy, 1558. Victoria and Albert Museum. MS. L. 2158/1947. In Italian. Vellum, 96 leaves. 10 × 7⅜ inches.

Laws and regulations to be observed by the procurators of the Church of S. Mark of Venice. Written in a precise and sloping *cancellaresca formata* with upright capitals. 22 lines to the full page. Rubricated in vermilion. The folios are in this colour. Square initials and surrounding arabesque decoration in matt (shell) gold set on squares of carmine and ultramarine alternately. On the page reproduced the background to letter D is blue. The first leaf of the actual text, which was probably decorated, is missing. This fact is noted here as it may have survived in some other collection. The last page carries the following colophon:

Presbyter Joannes de Vitalibus Brixiae scripsit, et literis au|reis celestinisq3 ornauit hunc librum Anno Domini M.D.LVIII.

42

LA PARAPHRASI by Flaminio.

Italy, *c.* 1545. British Museum. Harleian MS. 3541. In Italian. Vellum, 115 leaves. 8⅛ × 5⅛ inches.

Italian paraphrases of Psalms 1–42 by Marc Antonio Flaminio.

On the page reproduced here the title 'Sopra il terzo salmo etc' is in vermilion. The text is written over blind ruling in a very careful hand with almost typographic precision in the style of Ruano.[1] This seems to be the same hand as on Plate 43.

A paraphrase and commentary by the same author was published in Paris in 1549.

43

PANEGYRIC TO SULEIMAN THE MAGNIFICENT.

Italy, *c.* 1550. Harvard College Library. MS. Typ. 145 H. In Italian. Vellum, 10 leaves. 7½ × 5 inches.

This manuscript which seems to come from the same hand as Plate 42 has illuminated borders on each page. These show in small cameos scenes from the life of Sultan Suleiman.

[1] Another page of this manuscript was reproduced in *A Book of Scripts* by Alfred Fairbank.

44

A POLYGLOT PRAYER BOOK.

England, 1578. British Museum. Stowe MS. 30. In Italian. Vellum, 95 leaves. 6⅜ × 3⅞ inches.

Known as Queen Elizabeth's Prayer Book: 'Prayers in all Languages, Characters, Handwriting & Colers, presented to Queen Elizabeth.' The pages reproduced are from an Italian prayer: *Oratione del popolo*. We selected these two pages not so much for their quality as for the fact that they show in an unusually large size an italic which is after all mostly used as a small epistolarian hand.

The prayers in this book are in Greek, Latin, French, Italian, Spanish, German, Dutch, and Hebrew.

To quote Roger Ascham: 'Yea I beleue, that beside her perfit readines, in *Latin, Italian, French*, and *Spanish*, she (Queen Elizabeth) readeth here now at Windsore more Greeke euery day, than some Prebendarie of this Chirch doth read *Latin* in a whole weeke. And that which is most praise worthie of all, within the walles of her priuie chamber, she hath obtayned that excellencie of learnyng, to vnderstand, speake, and write, both wittely with head, and faire with hand, as scarce one or two rare wittes in both the Vniversities have in many yeares reached unto.' From *The Scholemaster*, 1570.

The first page of the manuscript is elaborately decorated with the royal arms in the centre and the date 1578 surrounded by the inscription 'Deus tuetur Reginam Elizabeth' and SIDEVS PRONOBIS / QVIS CŌRA NOS.

Bound in a contemporary binding in red velvet with ER embroidered on spine.

45

NAVIGATION. Writing attributed to Pierre Hamon.

France, *c.* 1560. British Museum. Harleian MS. 3996. In French. Vellum, 22 leaves. 8⅞ × 6½ inches.

The translator, Nicholas de Nicolay, also known as Nicolay d'Arfeuille Dauphinois, says that he has travelled in strange countries, even amongst Turks and barbares (Berbers, or barbarians ?). He had the good fortune, while staying at the court of Henry VIII of England, to meet his Admiral, the Duke of Northumberland.

This first known survey of the coast of Scotland was made by Alexander Lindsay, the pilot of the expedition, during a voyage of James V to the Hebrides. The title of the first French printed edition is: *La Navigation du Roy d'Escosse Jaque cinquiesme*, Paris, Gilles Beys 1583—with a chart.

According to the Foreword to the 1583 edition de Nicolay was helped with the translation from the original in the Scottish (en lãgage Escossois) by Maistre Jehan Ferrier, *tres-docte Escossois*. First time published in English as *Done from the French original, printed at Paris 1583* in *Miscellanea Antiqua*: containing first the Life and Death of King James the Vth of Scotland, etc. London, for W. Taylor at the Ship in Paternoster Row, 1720.

It can be assumed that there was originally an accompanying map. In the view of the present author this manuscript, which is dedicated to Charles, Cardinal de Lorraine, is in the hand of the famous French writing-master Pierre Hamon. It is intriguing to find in *Premier Volume de La Bibliotheque du Sieur de la Croix du Maine* (Paris, 1584): . . . *Pierre Hamon, natif de Bloys, secretaire de la chambre du Roy . . . cellui-cy estoit le plus renommé de France, voire de l'Europe, pour la perfection qu'il avoit d'escrire en toutes sortes de lettres. Il a fait imprimer plusieurs alphabetes ou livres d'Exemples réduits par ordre d'Abc, lesquels ont esté gravez. . . . Il a fait la description des Gaules en 12 Cartes, escrites de sa main sur parchemin, lesquelles il présenta à Monsieur le Révérendissime Charles Cardinal de Lorraine. Elles ne sont encore imprimées.*

This manuscript of which we show here the title-page only is worthy to be reproduced in full by a Scottish Society.

An early English manuscript of this book—if not the original—is listed in the Manuscript Catalogue of the Lumley library as: 'Alexander Lindesey his rutter of the sea, with havens, roades, soundes, etc., from Humber northwarde rownde about Scotland, anglice, manuscript.' No. 2505 Unidentified manuscript.

(Cf. p. 280 of The Lumley Library, the catalogue of 1609. Edited by Sears Jayne and Francis R. Johnson, B.M. 1956.)

46

A LETTER FROM CAMBRIDGE UNIVERSITY. Writing attributed to Bartholomew Dodington.

England, 1561. Public Record Office. S.P. 12/17, f. 10. In Latin. Paper. 12×8 inches.

To the Queen from Cambridge University. Prays for her protection in regard to their rights and privileges. 7 May 1561. Writing attributed to Bartholomew Dodington.

47

A LETTER WRITTEN BY BARTHOLOMEW DODINGTON.

England, 1561. Public Record Office. S.P. 12/20, No. 7. In Latin. Paper. 10¾×7⅝ inches.

To Cecil from Bartholomew Dodington. Requests his influence to be elected Public Orator. Cambridge. 15 October 1561.

Bartholomew Dodington (1536–90) was first at St. John's College, Cambridge, but later a Fellow of Trinity College and Regius Professor of Greek. He was also an Auditor of the Imprest.

The earliest letter written by him which has come to light is dated 1558 (P.R.O.— S.P. 12/2, f. 83) and this was written in the 'Cheke hand' (the script also shown in Plate 47), which he continued to use until at least 1586 as a more fluent hand than that of Plate 46. As Cheke died in 1557, Dodington may not have been under his direct influence, but John Strype records that Dodington was the companion of Cheke's son Henry (Dodington was twelve years older than Henry Cheke).

Dodington was a very consistent writer and the set script of 1590 shown in Plate 27 of 'A Book of Scripts' differs little from Plate 46 except in an assured and matured certainty of touch and design. When signing documents as Auditor his signature, in pointed italic, has always the precise distinction of his script. Like Roger Ascham, he appears to have written the Secretary hand. His writing of Greek is exquisite.

48

A LIST OF BENEFACTORS AND SCHOLARS OF TRINITY COLLEGE, CAMBRIDGE.

England, 1563. Public Record Office. S.P. 12/32, f. 3r. In Latin. Paper. 12¾×9 inches.

List of Founders, Benefactors, and Scholars of Trinity College Cambridge, 1563. A splendid and proud page written with great mastery of letter form and flourish.

Thomas Nashe says sixteen years later of Trinity College in his address *To the Gentlemen Students*, prefixed to *R. Greene's Menaphon*, 'that royall erection of Trinitie Colledge, which the Vniversitie Orator, in an epistle to the Duke of Somerset, aptlie termed *Colonia diducta* from the suburbes of Saint Johns', thus showing its spiritual dependence at that time on St. John's College.

This document reproduced here for the first time is, apart from its calligraphic quality, important because of its two initials C and H, which show that the Venetian Tagliente's book of 1524 was known to the academic Cambridge scribe. The initial letter H appears already in 1523 on p. 3 of Arrighi's *Il modo de temperare le penne* which significantly was also printed at Venice.

See also Plate 64, a broadsheet printed by Blado in 1534, for another use of this initial letter C.

49

A REMONSTRANCE FROM LA ROCHELLE.

France, 1573. British Museum. Lansdown MS. 18, f. 38. In Latin. Paper. $13 \times 9\frac{1}{2}$ inches.

Opening of a three-page letter in Latin written in a bluish ink: 'A Christian Remonstrance, from the Senate and people of La Rochelle, 1573', probably addressed to Burghley asking for support and touching a sum of money they had borrowed.

La Rochelle was a Huguenot stronghold for many years. As a seaport in the possession of friendly allies it was of considerable importance to Queen Elizabeth's government.

The editor of the Lansdown Catalogue of MSS., published by the British Museum in 1819, who does not usually offer comments on the quality of calligraphy, thought this document 'remarkable for the beauty of penmanship'. We concur and admire the regular flow of lines only pleasantly interrupted by the diagonal strokes of some letter forms as Q and R.

50

A LETTER FROM JOHN STILL.

England, 1579. British Museum. Lansdown MS. 28, f. 186. In Latin. Paper. $12\frac{1}{2} \times 9$ inches.

This letter is addressed on the outside as follows: 'Serenissima Principi Elisabethae Angliae Franciae et Hiberniae Reginae.' The original superscription summarizes the contents of the document thus: 'The Master and Fellows of Trinity College (Cambridge) to the Queen. Declaring how the request shee made to them for a certain Rectory to be bestowed upon one of their College was against their "statutes".'

The letter, dated 11 December 1579, was possibly written by John Still (1543?–1608) then Master of Trinity College. The Anthony Wingfield (1550–1615) mentioned is known as reader in Greek to Queen Elizabeth. Another letter survives (Lans. 28/192/3) written on the same day, by the same hand and with the same nine signatures but addressed to Burghley. 'The Masters and Fellows of Trinity, to Burghley; to back their letter and business to the Queen.'

The page of firm and skilled italic contains some lines of roman not less skilfully written: about 80 letters of roman to the line and about 100 letters of italic which demonstrates the compactness of the italic letter.

In writing an official letter like this, the scholar John Still achieves a professional scribe's competence.

51

A LETTER FROM JOHN PALMER.

England, 1581. British Museum. Lansdown MS. 33/38. In Latin. Paper. $12\frac{1}{4} \times 8$ inches.

Letter by John Palmer, a scholar of Westminster and Cambridge, to Lord Burghley, to procure him a fellowship, 2 September 1581. Beautifully written with initials in black and gold. Palmer became a Fellow of Trinity College, Cambridge, in 1582 and Archdeacon of Ely 1592–1600. He died in 1614.

We think he may have been a pupil of Peter Bales.

52

A LETTER FROM JOHN DEE.

England, 1588. British Museum. Harleian MS. 6986, f. 45. In English. Paper. $12 \times 7\frac{1}{2}$ inches.

Dr. John Dee (1527–1608) studied at St. John's College, Cambridge, and was famous as a mathematician and astrologer. His was a most colourful life. To mention only a few facts: some clever stage effects which he employed at a production in Cambridge of a play by Aristophanes earned him his life-long fame as a magician. He lectured on Euclid in Paris, suggested to Queen Mary the formation of a royal library of ancient manuscripts, travelled to Hungary, voyaged to St. Helena, drew hydrographical and geographical descriptions of newly discovered countries for Queen Elizabeth.

The letter to Queen Elizabeth here reproduced is written at the end of a four-years' stay in Bohemia, where he had at Prague audiences with the Emperor Rudolph II, the patron of Kepler and Tycho de Brahe.

He congratulates Queen Elizabeth on the defeat of the Spanish Armada and announces his and his family's return to England. The Mr. (Edward) Kelley mentioned in the letter was *Skryer* to the Doctor; he, however, separated from Dee and did not return.

This letter is mentioned in Dr. Dee's Diary in the following entry: 'Nov. 23rd, . . . I writ to the Queen's Majestie' (1588).

53

VIVAT SERENISSIMA ANGLIÆ REGINA.

Holland, 1590. British Museum. Lansdown MS. 66, f. 174. In Latin. Paper. 12¾×9 inches.

An enclosure to a letter from Captain George Wybrandt Bornstra to Queen Elizabeth. March 1590.

Written with all the skill and command of hand the Dutch writing-master could display in 'striking'. Clarity is maintained in spite of superimposition and intricacy of flourishes.

54

A LETTER FROM LADY LUCY ST. JOHN.

England, 1588. British Museum. Lansdown MS. 104, f. 175. In English. Paper. 12¼×9 inches.

A letter to Lord Burghley, from his 'obedyente' daughter; with an unnecessary apology for her 'bade writynge' (but she was unconscious of her bad spelling) and thanking him for his many favours. September 1588.

55

QUEEN ELIZABETH'S 'PRAYER AT THE GOING OUT OF HER NAVY'.

England, 1597. British Museum. Harleian MS. 6986, f. 58. In English. Paper. 5¾×7⅜ inches.

Believed to have been composed by Queen Elizabeth as a prayer for the safety of the ships under the command of the Earl of Essex which she dispatched in 1597 to scatter the Spanish fleet preparing to attack Ireland. Another version of this prayer was added, in a different hand, to the manuscript of Elizabeth's translation of 'The Mirror of the Sinful Soul' referred to in the note to Plate 28 and on page 32.

56

A LETTER WRITTEN BY LADY ARABELLA STUART.

England, 1605. British Museum. Harleian MS. 6986, f. 71. In English. Paper. 11 × 8 inches.

A letter to the then eleven-years-old Prince Henry by Arabella Stuart (1575–1615), daughter of Charles Stuart, Earl of Lennox, and niece of Lord Darnley, next heir to the English throne after her cousin James I and his children. She was secretly engaged to William Seymour who was also in the royal succession and married him in 1610. Died in the Tower.

Mr. (Adam) Newton and Sir David Murray mentioned in this letter were tutors to Prince Henry. This is the elegantly formal hand of Arabella Stuart. There are, however, letters in existence which were sent by her to the King from the Tower which look entirely different and are shorn of all calligraphic finery as written under great emotional stress.

57, 58, 59

LA OPERINA BY LUDOVICO ARRIGHI.

Italy, 1522.

IL MODO DE TEMPERARE LE PENNE BY LUDOVICO ARRIGHI.

Italy, 1523.

For many centuries handwriting had been taught by clerks and schoolmasters. Quite apart from their everyday teaching they sometimes put pen to paper or parchment to record their ABC's and examples of writing. Only very few of the medieval manuscripts containing such model styles of alphabets and specimens of scripts have survived. The advent of printing did not immediately engender writing copy-books. The first printed books were produced for people—mostly clergy—who could read and write.

The schoolmaster or the specialist writing-master diligently set his copy for his scholars and thus earned his livelihood. There was therefore no need for printed specimens of scripts.

In 1522 Ludovico degli Arrighi, called Vicentino, produced and published his writing manual—*La Operina,* &c.

This fine book is most important not only as *opus princeps* of its calligraphic kind but as a landmark in the literature of education.

He states in the address to the reader (p. 3 in the original edition) that asked by many friends and having regard for public use and benefit, not only in this age but also for posterity, he would give examples of the writing and formation of the characters which are called Cancellaresche; and as it was impossible for him to give enough examples written by his own hand, he has put them into print. He goes on to say that they are as close to his own handwriting as possible, but he wants to be excused if they do not answer in every small point; he is conscious of the fact that printing cannot represent entirely the living hand.

It needed more than an ordinary writing-master to bring out the first printed writing-book. The fact that he was once a publisher with knowledge of the printing of books, before becoming scriptor of apostolic briefs and skilful calligrapher of manuscripts, must have helped him to decide on this pioneer venture.

The arrangement of the lettering on the page is noble and elegant and the textual column conforms in its slender and tall measurement with the proportions of Arrighi's individual letters as seen on the same page. It is intriguing then to find this confirmed on page 7 of *La Operina* where he postulates that the basic form of the letter ought to be: *quadretto oblungo et non quadro perfetto*; an oblong parallelogram and not a complete square. A similar view was expressed by Cellini (see note to Plate 63).

60, 61

A ROYAL MANUSCRIPT ATTRIBUTED TO ARRIGHI.

Italy, *c.* 1520. British Museum. Royal MS. 12 C.VIII. In Latin. Vellum, 87 leaves. 8 × 5 inches.

Mr. Fairbank bases his attribution on the style and on comparison with the other three recognized Arrighi manuscripts in italic: the small prayer book at the Fitzwilliam (Plate 62*a*), the burned Trissino at the British Museum (Plate 62*b*), and the *Ethica* of Aristotle at the Universiteits Bibliotheek of Amsterdam. The newly ascribed manuscript so excels in decoration and illumination as to merit a place beside the *Ethica*, which was written in 1517 by Arrighi for Vittoria Colonna.

I am able to support this attribution not only by concurring with Mr. Fairbank's reasons for ascribing the manuscript to Arrighi but also by pointing out that the *Apologues* were afterwards, in 1526, printed by the same Arrighi, just as the

Sophonisba by Trissino was written and printed by him. For the printing of these *Apologues* Clement VII granted Arrighi exclusive rights for ten years.

The book to which the new ascription relates contains four Apologues by Pandolfo Collenuccio of Pesaro (1444–1504), namely 'Agenoria', 'Misopenes', 'Alithia', and 'Bombarda', and Dialogues from Lucian translated into Latin by Livius Guidoloctus of Urbino, namely 'De Raptu Europae', 'Galene et Panope', and 'De Paridis Iudicio'. It has illuminated initial letters and borders. This beautiful book was given to Henry VIII by Geoffrey Chamber on the latter's return from a journey to Italy. The scribe and illuminator must have been given detailed instructions to ensure production of a truly royal manuscript, one displaying in harmonious design some of the Tudor kingly and heraldic symbols. Thus we find the arms of Henry VIII supported by greyhound and dragon and encircled by the Garter, and elsewhere in the manuscript the Garter is again used as a decoration. Tudor roses are abundantly used as part of the border design. Geoffrey Chamber, who held several important appointments during the reign of Henry VIII, commissioned this manuscript specially in Rome for this presentation, and claims in his Introduction that he had 'taken care that it should be written in the most elegant style of writing whereby the reading of the book should be rendered more enjoyable still'. ('. . . curaui ut politissimis characteribus conscriberetur, Vt hoc ceu inuitamento quodā addito ad legendum librum allicerere.')

62a

FROM A BOOK OF HOURS. Writing attributed to Arrighi.

Italy, *c.* 1515. Fitzwilliam Museum, Cambridge. MS. J. 156. In Latin. Vellum, 125 leaves. $4\frac{1}{2} \times 2\frac{1}{2}$ inches.

Two pages from a small Book of Hours, written and possibly illuminated by Arrighi.

This is a delightfully written and decorated manuscript. Each of the Hours begins with a fine ornamented or floreated initial together with the title on a label. The leaves have signatures like those of a printed book: a, aı, aıı, &c. This is an interesting point, as Arrighi is known to have been engaged in the production of printed books as early as 1510.

The binding is of old red velvet. The manuscript was presented to the Fitzwilliam Museum by G. Sandar in 1892.

62b, c

(*b*) A FRAGMENT OF A *SOPHONISBA* MANUSCRIPT.

Italy, *c*. 1520. British Museum. Add. MS. 26783. In Italian. Vellum, 56 leaves. 5⅞×4 inches.

(*c*) ARRIGHI'S SECOND TYPE IN THE PRINTED EDITION OF *SOPHONISBA*.

Italy, 1524.

Sophonisba is a tragedy in blank verse composed by Giovanni Giorgio Trissino in 1514.

The marginal names of characters in the MS. are written in gold. An exquisite book written by Arrighi but badly damaged by fire.

It was first printed by Arrighi in his second italic type in 1524.

A copy of *Sophonisba* is listed in the manuscript Catalogue of the library of King James VI of Scotland (later James I of England) and is there described as '*un petit livret*'. Was it the identical manuscript from which we reproduce a fragment or was it a copy of the book printed by Arrighi of which we show here some lines from the last page (62*c*)? In 1611 Sir David Murray (1567–1629) published *The Tragical Death of Sophonisba*.

63

JANICULO'S TYPESHEET OF THE SECOND ITALIC TYPE OF ARRIGHI.

Italy, *c*. 1529. British Museum Library. C. 107.k.8. Paper. 11⅛×14½ inches.

The second type of Arrighi's was engraved after his design by the goldsmith and medallist, Lautitio di Meo de Rotelli of Perugia.

The integral fact in the association of Arrighi and the seal engraver Lautitio was that he, Lautitio, used punches for impressing the lettering on the matrices, from which seals were made. Punches also were required by Arrighi for the striking of matrices, that are essential for the casting of printing types. It is worth remembering here that Gutenberg came from a family connected with the mint of his native town, that Jenson was mint master at Tours and Caslon an engraver of gun barrels, before becoming a typefounder.

Benvenuto Cellini in his autobiography gives high praise to Lautitio:

'There was at that time in Rome a very able artist of Perugia named Lautizio, who worked only in one department, where he was sole and unrivalled throughout the world. You must know that at Rome every Cardinal had a seal, upon which his title is engraved, and these seals are made just as large as a child's hand of about twelve years of age; and, as I have already said, the Cardinal's title is engraved upon the seal with a great many ornamental figures. A well-made article of the kind fetches a hundred or more than a hundred crowns. This excellent workman . . . roused in me some honest rivalry, although the art he practised is far removed from the other branches of goldsmithery and consequently Lautizio was not skilled in making anything but seals.' (The *Life of Benvenuto Cellini* written by himself, Phaidon Press, 1949.)

Cellini elaborates this further in his Treatise on Goldsmithing, *Trattato dell' Oreficeria*, quoted here from C. R. Ashbee's translation, London, 1898.

'This sort of work is delightful. In my time in Rome, that was about 1525, there was a certain master from Perugia, called Lautizio, who practised nothing else but the making of seals for the bulls of cardinals. These seals are about the size of a ten-year-old child's hand and they are made in the shape of an almond. The cardinal's title is engraved on them, and usually in the form of a rebus, or allegorically. Lautizio used to get at least 100 scudi for each seal he made.'

In the following passage from the same book Cellini describes the engraver's use of punches in preparing the seal matrix. Arrighi was fortunate to get Lautitio, who was 'unrivalled throughout the world' in this art, to engrave his type and to strike the matrices with 'dexterous strokes'. The result we see on Plates 62*c* and 63.

'Now note this: my custom was to cut out the heads, hands and feet of my figures on small steel punches, and thinking the work came clearer and got a better result, I struck these punches with dexterous strokes upon the seal with a hammer into their different places. Also you should make in a similar manner an alphabet of steel punches . . . (likewise many other conceits according as taste prompts). When I was in Rome, or elsewhere, working in this like I oftimes amused myself by making new alphabets, each for its occasion, for they wear out soon, and I got much credit by my inventiveness. Your letters should be well formed, and shaped as a broadly cut pen might shape them; the strokes going up or down with the action of the hand, the letters being neither too fat and stumpy, nor too long and thin, for both these are unpleasing to behold, the moderately slim ones are the nicest to look at.'

This important passage describes beautifully the character of good lettering but has been overlooked so far by the historians of letter founding and therefore has been here quoted in full.

Gian Giorgio Trissino (1478–1550), the poet, was born at Vicenza. Arrighi came from the same town hence his *cognomen*, Vicentino. Arrighi printed six books for Trissino who was keenly interested in spelling reform, and added some Greek letters to the alphabet that was cut by Lautitio Perusino for Arrighi.

When Trissino left Rome for his home town, Vicenza, he took with him a set of strikes of Arrighi's type and set up Tolomeo Janiculo there as his printer.

Janiculo's broadsheet reproduced here shows the various letter combinations and his splendid colophon.

For Trissino's influence in England see note to Plate 26.

This type was revived by Frederic Warde in 1925 and used for the first time for the printing of *Crito, A Socratic Dialogue by Plato. Translated by Henry Cary*, Paris, The Pleiad Press, 1926.

The imprint reads: 475 copies printed for the Pleiad under the supervision of Frederic Warde being the first use of a new type, by the Officina Bodoni, Montagnola, Switzerland, 1926.

The type (cut by Charles Malin of Paris) was also used in the same year for the introduction to the facsimile edition of Arrighi's writing-books, also printed by the Officina Bodoni for Frederic Warde. A notable use was made of this type in Douglas Cleverdon's edition of *The Ancient Mariner* by Coleridge, illustrated with engravings by David Jones and printed by Ernest Ingham at the Fanfare Press in 1929.

64

A BROADSHEET SHOWING THE THIRD ITALIC TYPE OF ARRIGHI.

Italy, 1534. British Museum Library. C. 18. e. 2, f. 29. Paper. $18\frac{5}{8} \times 13$ inches.

'Anglici Matrimonii. Sententia diffinitiva.' Broadsheet announcement of the final decision concerning the English marriage: in favour of Catherine of Aragon and against Henry VIII. Rome, 23 March 1534. The document is signed Blosius.[1]

It is printed in Arrighi's third type by Antonio Blado,[2] who was printer to the Apostolic See from 1528 to 1567. The initial letter C, however, can be traced back to Tagliente's manual. In this third type Arrighi has produced a more workmanlike

[1] Blosius Palladius, Latin Secretary to Clement VII and editor of *Coryciana*, the first printed book to be issued from Arrighi's *Officina* (July 1524). For briefs signed by Blosius, see B.M. Cotton MS., Vitellius B. XI.

[2] G. Fumagalli in *Antonio Blado, Tipografo Romano* mentions an item printed by Blado two years earlier: *Consultationes Jurisconsultorum Italiae in causa matrimoniali inter Henricum VIII Angliae regem & Catharinam Reginam*.

letter than his two previous designs. In contrast to the more calligraphic treatment of his first and second types, the ascenders and descenders of this third type go straight up or down; in other words the same finials are used as in roman type. Apart from the ligatures the italic letters used by Aldus Manutius for his pocket size classics from 1501 onwards show similar characteristics. Arrighi first used this new type in 1526 for the printing of a book in Pandolpho Collenuccio's *Speculo di Esopo.*

Scaccia Scarafonte[1] described and reproduced an indulgence from 8 June 1527 in which absolution is granted to the Imperial Army who had already been sacking Rome for many weeks. At the same time the Pope was made to pay a ransom of 400,000 ducats and furthermore to grant certain territorial concessions.

The printing of this indulgence was executed in the same type of Arrighi's, whose last work it may have been. It is very likely that he perished during the events of 1527. These monstrous conditions were extorted from the Pope by the general in command of the army of the Emperor Charles V who was a nephew of Catherine of Aragon. Charles V took up her cause later when Clement VII was asked by Henry VIII for the grant of a divorce from his Queen.

One cannot resist the feeling that Catherine's relationship with the Holy Roman Emperor, whose troops could inflict such terrible disaster as the Sack of Rome, carried considerably more weight than the application of the more remote King Henry, Defender of the Faith.

This is one instance where small specimens of typography can perhaps contribute to our understanding of the course of important historical events.

65

(*a*) FROM A SUPPLICATION WRITTEN BY TAGLIENTE.

Italy, 1491. Archivio di Stato, Venice.

(*b*) *LO PRESENTE LIBRO INSEGNA.*

Italy, 1524.

Giovanantonio Tagliente appears first on the calligraphic scene in his supplication to the Doge and Council of Venice in 1491, the last few lines of which are shown in this Plate.[2]

[1] In *Bibliofilia*, xl, Jan., Feb. 1938, pp. 48–53.   [2] First described by James Wardrop in *Signature*.

The fact that Arrighi Vicentino came in 1523 from Rome to complete and print his second manual in Venice may well have stirred the much older Tagliente into that activity which resulted in the producing and publishing of his own manual by the following year. A link between Arrighi's second book and Tagliente's manual was the collaboration of Eustachio Celebrino as engraver for both. That may explain the appearance of the same ABC of interlaced Lombardic capitals and the use of a decorative initial letter H in both books.

The first edition of Tagliente's manual, from which we reproduce a page, has the following title:

'Lo presente libro Insegna La Vera arte delo Excellẽ / te scriuere de diuerse varie sorti di litere etc. Opera del tagliente nouamente / composta cum gratia nel anno di ñra salute / 1524.' Venice.

Tagliente's book was very popular, appearing in many editions, and was even copied in Antwerp in 1545 by Johannes Loëus.

66

THESAVRO DE SCRITTORI BY SIGISMUNDO FANTI.

Italy, 1535.

Title-page of one of the many recorded editions of *Thesauro de Scrittori*, first published in 1525. This book was printed by Blado in Rome and produced by Ugo da Carpi, who was an engraver of wood-blocks, famous for his experiments in the *chiaroscuro* technique of printing from different coloured tone blocks.

The book is made up of copies of parts of Arrighi, Tagliente, and Sigismundo Fanti. Fanti, a nobleman from Ferrara, according to the title, was an architect and mathematician. It is said that Ugo da Carpi cut *La Operina* by Arrighi on wood. Nobody knows why, but the fact remains, that in 1525 the Pope granted Ugo the right to print *La Operina*.

67

SETTE ALPHABETI DI VARIE LETTERE BY FERDINANDO RUANO.

Italy, 1554.

Ferdinando Ruano, a Spaniard by birth, worked from 1541 to 1560 at the Vatican Library as, to use his own expressions, *Scriptor Bibliothecae Apostolicae Vaticanae* or *Scriptor della libraria*. His book contains several alphabets and shows their construction with ruler and compass. The geometric formation and planning of letter forms had become a craze in the sixteenth century. It goes back as far as we know to Felice Feliciano and to the sound construction of capital letters shown in the book printed in *c.* 1480 by Damianus Moyllus of Parma.

The awakened interest in perspective and mathematics made people try the near impossible, in this case the superimposition of geometric lines over the freely formed letters of the italic script. Nevertheless, we find Ruano's book important as it shows on a large scale an upright cancellaresca that, being conveniently perpendicular in its downstrokes, fits easily in the net of vertical and horizontal lines. The curved pen marks of the italic, however, being based on an oval and not a circular pattern seem to be too complicated for the quick circumscription of the compass.

68*a*, *b*, 69*a*

A SPECIMEN BOOK WRITTEN BY PALATINO.

Italy, *c.* 1540. Bodleian Library, Oxford. MS. Canon Ital. 196, f. 36, f. 44, and f. 56. In Italian. Vellum, 87 leaves. 6⅞×9¼ inches.

69*b*, 70*a*, *b*

LIBRO NUOVO D'IMPARARE A SCRIVERE TUTE SORTE LETTERE BY PALATINO.

Italy, 1540.

Palatino's copy-book 'LIBRO NVOVO / D'IMPARARE A SCRIVERE TV / TE SORTE LETTERE ANTICHE ET MO / DERNE DI TVTTE NATIONI, / CON NVOVE REGOLE / MISVRE ET ES / SEMPI / Con vn breue & vtile trattato de le Cifere, Composto per / Giouambattista Palatino Cittadino Romano, . . . Rome 1540' (Plates 69*b*, 70*a* and *b*) was as popular in his time as Tagliente's. Complementary to it, is the collection of examples in a manuscript written on vellum now at the Bodleian Library of which three are reproduced here (Plates 68*a*, 68*b*, and 69*a*). Plate 68 shows the *Cancellaresca formata* and Plate 68*b* shows *Cancellaresca corsiva*, Plate 69*a* a display not only of swash capitals in variety but also the contractions of address, very useful at the time to Italian letter-writers.

Plate 69*b* from the printed manual shows a loss of calligraphic crispness sustained through the process of wood engraving and overinking. Nevertheless, it provides an interesting comparison with the writing above.

71, 72, 73

GERARD MERCATOR'S WRITING MANUAL.

Flanders, 1540.

Literarum Latinarum, quas Italicas, cursoriasque vocant, scribendarum ratio. Antwerp, 1540.

The title of the 1557 edition describes Mercator as *Authore et sculptore* which proves that he was not only the scribe and author but also the engraver of the wood-blocks from which his book was printed.

Mercator's fame is based on his reputation as an engraver of maps and maker of globes, but in this treatise, which is itself written in Latin, he propagates the use of a cursive italic for the penning of Latin letters.

Mercator's text contains careful instruction as to the cutting of quills and for the shaping of every detail of letter form. Two woodcuts show how to and how not to hold a pen.

This manual may well have found its way to England, and because it was written entirely in Latin should have appealed to the schoolmasters teaching that language more than copies of Arrighi and Tagliente reprinted in Flanders about the same time.

We should not fail to mention here that Gerard Mercator had in common with Arrighi that singularity of purpose to dedicate an entire book to the expounding of one style of writing.

One can well imagine how suitable Mercator must have found this *littera italica* in his own cartographic work. The compressed character of the letter enabled him to fit long topographical names into confined spaces and the flourishes became very decorative in the open spaces of seas and deserts.

74

A WRITING MANUAL BY CASPAR NEFF.

Germany, 1549.

From *Thesaurium Artis Scriptoriae* or *Eine Köstliche Schatzkammer der Schreibkunst* by Caspar Neff, Cologne 1549.

'Une Escripture Francoyse, laquelle on use en La Chancellerie.' A pleasant French Chancery italic here shown in a German manual many years before the publication of the first French copy-book.

75

A MANUSCRIPT BY VESPASIANO AMPHIAREO.

Italy, 1548. Harvard College Library. Vellum, 20 leaves. 7×10 inches.

76, 77

OPERA . . . NELLA QUALE SI INSEGNA A SCRIVERE BY VESPASIANO
AMPHIAREO.

Italy, 1554.

Not every writing-master produced a printed manual, but in the course of teaching
they prepared specimen leaves for individual pupils. Sometimes these samplars
were collected and published.

Plate 75 is from a manuscript without title which is signed *fr. Vespasianus Amphya-
reus Ferrarese*. This calligrapher was born at Ferrara in 1501 and died in 1563. According to the dedication of his printed manual (1554 edition) he had begun his teaching
in 1524.

Amphiareo produced one printed manual, first published in Venice in 1548, which
went through many editions. It is interesting to find that on fol. 5v. of the Harvard
MS. he records that he was then supervising the printing of a writing manual.

78, 79, 80

ARTE SUBTILISSIMA BY JUAN DE YCIAR.

Spain, 1548. Other editions, 1550, 1553, 1555, &c.

'Recopila|cion subtilissima: inti|tulada Orthographia | practica: por la qual se
enseña a escreuir per|fectamente: ansi por practica como por geome|tria todas las
suertes de letras que mas en nue|stra España y fuera della se vsan. | Hecho y experi-
mentado por Iuā de Yciar Vizcayno, | escriptor de libros. Y cortado por | Iuan de
Vingles Frances. | Es materia de si muy prouechosa para toda calidad | de personas
que eneste exercicio se qui | sieren exercitar. | Impreso en Caragoca, por Bartholo |
mede Nagera M.D.XL.VIII. 4º.'

Yciar is described by Mori as *El patriarca y fondador de la caligrafia española*. The first
edition of 1548 shows a portrait of the author at the age of twenty-five. From this

we conclude that he was born in 1522 or 1523, at Durango in the province of Vizcayo. The title-page displays in lunette-rounded arch the author in the attitude of writing an alphabet. He mentions in his book Palatino, Vicentino, Tagliente, and others.

One cannot help feeling that in all their elegance the Spanish italics of Yciar, Lucas, and Brun, and the Italian of Amphiareo, with their parallelism of lines, owe something to the Gothic tradition.

It may be an exaggeration to state, as El. Herm. Lorenço Ortiz does, in his *Maestro de Escribir*, 'Los Espanoles han sido los mejores escribanos del mundo', but there can be no doubt that Yciar's book has to be counted amongst the finest calligraphic copy-books to be found anywhere at any time.

It seems that Yciar, the writing-master and scribe of service books, only supplied the pieces of lettering which, splendid as they are on their own, are much enhanced by the surrounding borders, decorations, and background. The fact that these are conspicuously signed with the name or initials of Jean de Vingles does suggest that de Vingles must have been in this case more than the jobbing wood engraver. It is interesting to find that Jean de Vingles belonged to a family of Lyons printers. See A. Claudin, *Les Antécédents d'Henry Poyvre et de Jean de Vingles*. He was the youngest son of his namesake who came from Picardy and worked in Lyons from 1494 to 1511. His eldest brother, Pierre de Vingles, dit Pirot Picard, went to Switzerland where he printed at Geneva and Neuchâtel.

Among other books the latter printed the first protestant Bible in French of the Olivetan version. If his brother Jean did not bring Bibles to Spain, he at least in Yciar's writing-book helped to make the art of fine writing more widely known there. The brothers had this in common that they used the device of their father's printer's mark of *un cœur surmonté d'une couronne*. See Silvestre, *Marques typographiques*, Nos. 205 and 435. This crowned heart device with the initials J.D.V. can be found on the title-page and on many pages of Yciar's 'Recopilacion Subtilissima. . . .'

81, 82, 83, 84

ARTE DE ESCREUIR BY FRANCISCO LUCAS.

Spain, 1571 and 1577.

Cotarelo y Mori describes Francis Lucas as the creator of *la letra bastarda española*. Lucas was born at Seville in the 1530's; he came to Madrid in 1570. His first writing book appeared in Toledo in 1571. The second one from which we reproduce as well was printed in Madrid in 1577. We give here in full the text of both titles:

1. 'Instrvccion / mvy provechosa para aprender a es / creuir, con auiso particular de la traça y hechura / de las letras de Redondilla y Bastarda, y de otras co / sas para bien escreuir necessarias. Hecha por Francisco Lucas maestro de enseñar a escreuir na / tural de la ciudad de Sevilla. / Dirigido al Mvy Illvstre S. Don / Diego de Castilla Dean y Canonigo de la sancta / Iglesia de Toledo. / En Toledo. / Por Francisco de Guzman. Año de M.D. LXXj / con privilegio Real. / Impresso en Toledo en casa / de Francisco de Guz / man Año De / 1571.'

2. 'Francisco Lucas

   Arte / de escreuir de / Francisco Lucas. / vezino de Seuilla, residente en corte de su Magestad / Diuidada en quarto partes. / Dirigida a la S.C.R.M. / Del Rey don Phellippe. II. / Nuestro Señor. / Con privilegio. / En Madrid, / En casa de Alonso Gomez, Impressor de sa Magestad 1577.'

   Further editions: 1580, 1608.

85

THE WRITING-BOOK OF ANDRES BRUN.

Spain, 1612.

'Arte muy provechoso / para apprender / de escrivir / perfectamente. / Hecho y experimentado por el Maestro Andres Brun Infancon / vezino y natural de la Ciudad de Saragoça con licencia. / En Saragoça, Por Iuant de la rumbe. / Año de M. DC. XII.'

This is the largest copy-book known to us ($12 \times 8\frac{1}{2}$ inches). The lettering is cut on planks of wood by the author himself. Some of the blocks are very large, but the page which we reproduce shows four small and narrow ones. Other pages are made up similarly, and may go back to his first specimens, published in 1583.

On the other hand certain plates show one line of an alphabet at the head of the page, the rest of the page is given over to ruled lines, for the pupil to copy his ABC. I assume the writing-master Brun had these pages printed separately and sold them to his scholars. Even the small narrow blocks may have been used at the head of otherwise blank writing-sheets.

Brun lived in Saragossa as did Yciar, but his work shows a strong influence of Lucas.

86

GIANFRANCESCO CRESCI'S 'PERFECT SCRIBE'.

Italy, 1570.

'IL PERFETTO SCRITTORE Di M. Gio. Francesco Cresci Cittadino Melanese. Doue si veggono i veri Caratteri, & le natural forme di tutte quelle sorti di lettere che a vero scrittor si appartengono. Con alcun' altre da lui nuouamente ritrouate. Et i modi, che deue tenere il mastro per ben insegnare.' Rome 1570. Cresci considered himself an innovator. In the introduction to this book he says that he has striven for many years to rediscover the true way of writing the *Cancellaresca Corsiva* more prettily and more quickly than the hand which was then in use; and besides this to find again many other lovely and more fugitive letters.

The plates were engraved by Giovan Francesco Aureri da Crema. One can say that Cresci tried to formalize certain tendencies to write with pressure and to use superficial formulas and blobs. Cresci's work has been treated by James Wardrop in *Signature*, No. 5, N.S. (1948) and by Sir Francis Meynell in the first issue of the *Bulletin of the Society of Italic Handwriting* (1954).

87

A WRITING-BOOK BY HERCOLANI.

Italy, 1574.

'Lo Scrittor' Vtile | et brieue Segretario | Da me Giuliantonio Hercolani.' 1574.

Copper engraving was a medium used first in Italy for book illustrations, maps, patterns of ornaments, and prints generally. It is therefore not surprising that this method of reproduction was employed for a copy-book. The plates were engraved in 1571 but the dates were altered to 1574 when the book was published.

88*a*

A SPECIMEN BOOK WRITTEN BY J. DE BEAUCHESNE.

? England, *c.* 1570. In English, French, Italian, and Latin. Vellum, 15 leaves. $4\frac{1}{4} \times 7\frac{1}{8}$ inches.

A page from a recently discovered calligraphic copy-book manuscript on vellum by 'Jehan de Beau Chesne', written *c.* 1570, in B. L. W.'s possession.

Beauchesne was born in Paris in 1538. He was a Huguenot and fled from his country to England. He settled in London at the age of twenty-seven. Five years later, in 1570, he produced, together with John Baildon, the first English writing-book.

In this Anthology we have been able to show autograph as well as printed exemplars and to these intriguing comparative plates of Renaissance writing-masters we add, and conclude with, an original showing of the writing of Beauchesne.

88*b*

THE FIRST ENGLISH WRITING-BOOK.

England, 1570.

'A booke containing divers sortes of hands as well the English as French secretarie with the Italian, Roman, Chancelry and Court hands. Also the true & iust proportiō of the capitall Romāē set forth by John de Beau Chesne. P. and M. Iohn Baildon.

'Imprinted at London by Thomas Vautrouillier, dwelling in the blacke frieres. 1570.'

The sixty plates of this book were cut on wood and with a certain homely quality give a perfect picture of the whole range of the Elizabethan period's calligraphic material.

89

ODES OF HORACE WRITTEN AND ILLUMINATED BY WILLIAM MORRIS.

England, 1874. Bodleian Library. MS. Lat. Class. e. 38, p. 42. In Latin. Vellum. $6\frac{5}{8} \times 4\frac{1}{2}$ inches.

William Morris's first calligraphic experiments began in 1857. Between 1870 and 1875 he wrote and illuminated several manuscripts; amongst these is the Horace, now at the Bodleian, from which we show a page.

Morris based his script mainly on humanist models, some of which he studied at the British Museum: see note to Plate 5.

He wrote on paper, and also on parchment, which Fairfax Murray got for him in Rome.

'. . . one notes importantly that at this period he had not wearied of the Renaissance. These MSS. show little of the Gothic tendencies of later book work; but the Renaissance methods are fresh as all his work is fresh, with an originality which has probed to the essential bottom of the business and then bursts upwards again with irrepressible vitality.' This quotation is from *The Illuminated MSS of William Morris* by Graily Hewitt, one of three papers, the others on W. M.'s typography by Holbrook Jackson and James Shand; read before the Double Crown Club. Privately printed. 1934.

90

A NEW HANDWRITING FOR TEACHERS BY MRS. M. M. BRIDGES.

England, 1896.

An introduction, some instructions on the use of the copies, and nine plates of models by Mrs. Bridges, one plate of a sixteenth-century hand by an anonymous writer, and one plate of Michael Angelo's careful handwriting.

This book is the first to instruct in a handwriting different from the copperplate derivatives generally taught in schools, which had become rather stale by the end of the Victorian era. Mrs. Bridges says in the Introduction to her book: '. . . I was always interested in handwriting, and after making acquaintance with the Italianised Gothic of the sixteenth century, I consciously altered my hand towards some likeness with its form and general character.' The interest of Robert Bridges is evident in a specimen of his writing as early as 1879 (*vide* p. 227 of *Poems and Prose of Gerard Manley Hopkins*, Penguin Books, 1954). It is known that in March 1891 Mrs. Bridges was 'doing some samples of handwriting which her husband hoped would be facsimiled and published'. But at that time it had not been decided about the most convenient form of some of the capitals. Edward Johnston was encouraged at the outset of his career by the Bridges, e.g. a copy of Maunde Thompson's *Palaeography* was given to him by Mrs. Bridges in August 1899. It has marginal notes by E. J. and is in the possession of A. F.

91 *a, b*

(*a*) WRITING BY EDWARD JOHNSTON.

England, 1924.

(*b*) WRITING BY GRAILY HEWITT.

England, 1916.

(*a*) An example of semi-formal writing illustrating an article 'The Cursive Hand' by Beatrix Holmes. *The Beacon*, vol. iii, No. 30, April 1924.

(*b*) An illustration from *Handwriting: Everyman's Handicraft*, Chiswick Press, 1916.

92

A LETTER WRITTEN BY MR. STANLEY MORISON.

England, 1932.

According to Mr. Stanley Morison, he was asked one day, actually it was the 5th of April 1932, by Mr. C. E. Carrington to write a few lines for the Cambridge University Press to be shown in E. E. Reynolds's book *Junior Exercises in English*. He wrote it 'clean off, there and then' and it shows an admirable combination of freedom and form.

93 a, b

WRITING CARDS BY ALFRED FAIRBANK.

England, 1932 and 1935.

(*a*) Woodside Writing Card No. 4. Dryad Press, 1932. (Out of print.)

(*b*) Barking Writing Card No. 7. Dryad Press, 1935. (The Barking Writing Cards were renamed Dryad Writing Cards. They were originally intended for use in schools at Barking.)

94

A LETTER WRITTEN BY MR. PAUL STANDARD.

United States, 1956.

Mr. Standard has for many years led the movement in the United States for the reform of handwriting by the adoption of the italic system.

95

ARRIGHI TRANSCRIBED.

England, 1956.

A translation and transcription of a page of Arrighi's manual *La Operina* by Miss Anna Hornby. Written with her left hand.

96

A CHEERFUL FINALE.

Written by a girl of eight whom we have been unable to identify.

BIBLIOGRAPHY OF
CONTEMPORARY WORKS

SIR EDWARD MAUNDE THOMPSON, *Introduction to Greek and Latin Palaeography*. Oxford University Press. 1912.

PROFESSOR B. L. ULLMAN, *Ancient Writing and its Influence*. George G. Harrap & Co. 1932.

N. DENHOLM-YOUNG, *Handwriting in England and Wales*. University of Wales Press. 1954.

L. C. HECTOR, *The Handwriting of English Documents*. Edward Arnold Ltd. 1958.

SIR HILARY JENKINSON, *The Later Court Hands in England, from the Fifteenth to Seventeenth Century*. Cambridge University Press. 1927.

LEWIS F. DAY, *Penmanship of XVI, XVII, and XVIII Centuries*. B. T. Batsford.

SIR AMBROSE HEAL, *The English Writing Masters and their Copy-books*. Introduction on the Development of Handwriting by Stanley Morison. Cambridge University Press. 1931.

JAN TSCHICHOLD, *An Illustrated History of Writing and Lettering*. Zwemmer. 1947.

ALFRED FAIRBANK, *A Book of Scripts*. Penguin Books Ltd. 1949.

E. A. LOWE, 'Handwriting'. Included in *The Legacy of the Middle Ages*. Oxford University Press. 1926.

STANLEY MORISON, 'Calligraphy'. Article in the *Encyclopaedia Britannica*. 14th edition.

EDWARD STRANGE, *Alphabets*. George Bell & Sons. 1898.

A. F. JOHNSON, A Catalogue of Italian Writing-books of the Sixteenth Century'. *Signature*, No. 10, N.S., 1950.

DON EMILIO COTARELO Y MORI, *Diccionario biográfico y bibliográfico de calígrafos españoles*, Madrid, 1913.

STANLEY MORISON. Articles in *The Fleuron*.

STANLEY MORISON, 'Early Humanistic Script and the First Roman Type', *The Library*, 4th ser., vol. xxiv, September 1943.

STANLEY MORISON, *Latin Script since the Renaissance*. Privately printed at the Cambridge University Press. 1938.

JAMES WARDROP. Articles in *Signature*:

'Arrighi Revived.' *Signature*, No. 12, July 1939.

'Pierantonio Sallando and Girolamo Pagliarolo, Scribes to Giovanni II Bentivoglio.' *Signature*, No. 2, N.S., November 1946.

'The Vatican Scriptors: Documents for Ruano and Cresci.' *Signature*, No. 5, N.S., 1948.

'A Note on Giovanantonio Tagliente.' *Signature*, No. 8, N.S., 1949.

'Civis Romanus Sum: Giovanbattista Palatino and His Circle.' *Signature*, No. 14, N.S., 1952.

JAMES WARDROP, 'Notes on Six Italian Manuscripts in the Department of Graphic Arts of Harvard College Library'. *Harvard Library Bulletin*, vol. vii, No. 2, Spring 1953.

JOHN P. ELDER, 'Clues in Dating Florentine Humanistic Manuscripts'. *Studies in Philology*, vol. xliv, April 1947.

ARNOLD BANK, 'Calligraphy & its Influence in the Time of Plantin'. Included in the *Memorial Volume of the Plantin Celebration 1555–1955*. Antwerp, 1956.

BERTHOLD WOLPE, 'A Royal Manuscript by Arrighi Vicentino in the British Museum'. Article in *The Book Collector*. Spring, 1958.

JACOB BURCKHARDT, *The Civilisation of the Renaissance in Italy*. Phaidon Press. 1944.
R. WEISS, *Humanism in England during the Fifteenth Century*. Basil Blackwell, Oxford. 1941.

The Calligraphic Models of Ludovico degli Arrighi surnamed Vicentino. A complete Facsimile and an Introduction by Stanley Morison. Privately printed for Frederic Warde. 1926.
Andres Brun: Calligrapher of Saragossa. Henry Thomas and Stanley Morison. Pegasus Press, Paris. 1929.
The Treatise of Gerard Mercator, Literarum Latinarum quas Italicas, cursoriasque vocant, scribendarum ratio (Antwerp, 1540). The Pegasus Press, Paris. 1930.
Opera di Tagliente, 1525. Reproduced in Facsimile with an Introduction by James M. Wells. The Newberry Library, Chicago. 1952.
Three Classics of Italian Calligraphy. An Unabridged Reissue of the Writing Books of Arrighi, Tagliente, and Palatino, with an Introduction by Oscar Ogg and a Bibliography by A. F. Johnson. Dover Publications, Inc., New York. 1953.
The First Writing Book. An English Translation and Facsimile text of Arrighi's *Operina*, the first manual of the Chancery hand, with Introduction and Notes by John Howard Benson. Yale University Press. 1954.
JUAN DE YCIAR. A facsimile edition of *Arte Subtilissima*, with introduction by Reynolds Stone and translation by Evelyn Shuckburgh. Lion & Unicorn Press. 1958.
A Newe Booke of Copies, 1574. A Facsimile of a Unique Elizabethan Writing Book in the Bodleian Library, Oxford. Edited, with an Introduction and Notes by Berthold Wolpe. Lion & Unicorn Press. 1959.
LUDOVICO VICENTINO. Facsimile of *La Operina & Il Modo de Temperare le Penne*, with articles by Sten G. Lindberg, Valter Falk, Stig-Åke Möller, and Gustaf Nordlander. Tidens Förlag, Stockholm. 1958.
The Instruments of Writing. Translated from the writing book of Giovanbattista Palatino, Rome, 1540, by the Reverend Henry K. Pierce. Berry Hill Press, Newport, R.I. 1954.

English Handwriting. Society for Pure English Tracts, Nos. XXIII (1926) and XXVIII (1927). Edited by Robert Bridges with notes by him and by Roger Fry, E. A. Lowe, and Alfred Fairbank. Oxford University Press.
PAUL STANDARD, *Calligraphy's Flowering, Decay, and Restauration*. Sylvan Press. 1947.
AUBREY WEST, *Written by Hand*. George Allen & Unwin Ltd. 1951.
WILFRID BLUNT, *Sweet Roman Hand*. James Barrie. 1952.
Lettering of To-day. Studio Ltd. 1937.
Italic Handwriting. Some Examples of Everyday Cursive Hands, selected by Wilfrid Blunt and Will Carter. Newman Neame Ltd. 1954.
The Bulletin of the Society of Italic Handwriting. A quarterly edited by Dr. W. N. Littlejohns. First issue, 1954.
The Calligrapher's Handbook. Essays by members of the Society of Scribes and Illuminators. Edited by C. M. Lamb. Faber & Faber Ltd. 1956.

M. M. BRIDGES, *The New Handwriting*. Oxford University Press. 1898.
EDWARD JOHNSTON, *Writing & Illuminating, & Lettering*. John Hogg. 1906.
GRAILY HEWITT, *The Oxford Copy-books*, Nos. 1 and 2. Oxford University Press. 1916.
ALFRED FAIRBANK, *A Handwriting Manual*. Faber & Faber Ltd. (Revised 1954.)
ALFRED FAIRBANK, *The Woodside Writing Cards*. Dryad Press, Leicester. 1932.
ALFRED FAIRBANK, *The Dryad Writing Cards*. Dryad Press, Leicester. 1935.
ALFRED FAIRBANK, CHARLOTTE STONE, and WINIFRED HOOPER. *Beacon Writing Books*. Ginn & Co. Ltd. 1958.

INDEX

Bold figures refer to plate numbers

PLATES

MANUSCRIPTS AND LETTERS

I

tanto melior angelis effectus quanto differen
tius prae illis nomen hereditauit · Cui enim dixit
aliquando angelorum filius meus es tu · ego hodie
genuite ? Et rursum ego ero illi in patre · et
ipse erit mihi in filium · Et cum iterum introducit
primogenitum in orbem terrae dicit · Et adorent
eum omnes angeli di̅ · Et ad angelos quide̅ dicit
Qui facit angelos suos sp̅s̅ · et ministros suos flam
mam ignis · Ad filium aut̅ · Thronus tuus d̅s̅ in
se̅c̅l̅m̅ se̅c̅l̅i · Et uirga aequitatis uirga regni tui ·

1. From Alcuin's Bible. Caroline minuscule. 9th century

2a, b. *Cicero: De Oratore*. Writing by Poggio. 1428

2c. *Ammianus Marcellinus*. Writing by Niccolò Niccoli

ceteris i predijs in melius in manib̄ uetus sane et angu
stia cū sit aliquid cū statio die freqtissima. Nam idi
bus septembribus magnus est e egurie tota ore populg.
multe ces aguntur. multa uota suscipuntur. multa
redduntur. Sed nullū in proximo suffragiu. aut imbris
aut solis uidero ego munifice simul religiose q̄ factu
rus. si eadem q̄ pulcherrima extruxero. addidero por
ticus edi illa aduersum deo has ad hom̄. Velim ergo
emas quatuor marmoreas collumnas cuis tibi uide
bitur gn̄is emas marmora quibus solū quibz̄ parie
tes extolantur. Erit etiā faciunda ipius deē signū
quia antiquū illud e ligno quibusdā uetustate sui
partibus truncatū est quantū ad porticus nihil inter
occurrit necesse repetendu. nisi tamen ut formā sc d
ratione loci scribas. neq̄ eim possum excudere templo
Nam solum templi hinc flumie et abruptissimis ripis
hinc uia cingitur. Est ultra uia latissima prati. in
quo satis apte gn̄ templū inuenes qui solent locorū dis
ficultates arte superare. Vale.

SCRIBIS pergratas tibi fuisse Lras meas
quibus cognouisti q̄ ad modū tuis oti esta
tis exegerem requiris quid ex hoc in Laurentino hyeme
p̄mutem. nihil nisi q̄ meridianus somn̄s eximitur
multu q̄ de nocte uel ante uel post diem sumitur et
si agendi necessitas instat que frequens hyeme uo ia
cōcedo uel lyriste p̄ cena loc̄s illa q̄ dēo ut idēdē re
tractat̄ ac sit memorie freqti emdaro pficiatur. has
estate hyeme consuetudine nō addas huc licet. rete
ti ūique iter hyemē star̄ estate q̄ media ut nihil de
die perdat de nocte parcius acquirat. Vale. deus Laudet

C PLINII SECVNDI VERONENSIS
ORATORIS EPTARVM LIBER VIII
ET VLTIMVS EXPLICIT IHS
ANNO DOMINI MCCCCLV

3. A page of a Pliny. Anonymous scribe. 1455

4. From a funeral oration. Writing by Marcus de Cribellaris. 1478

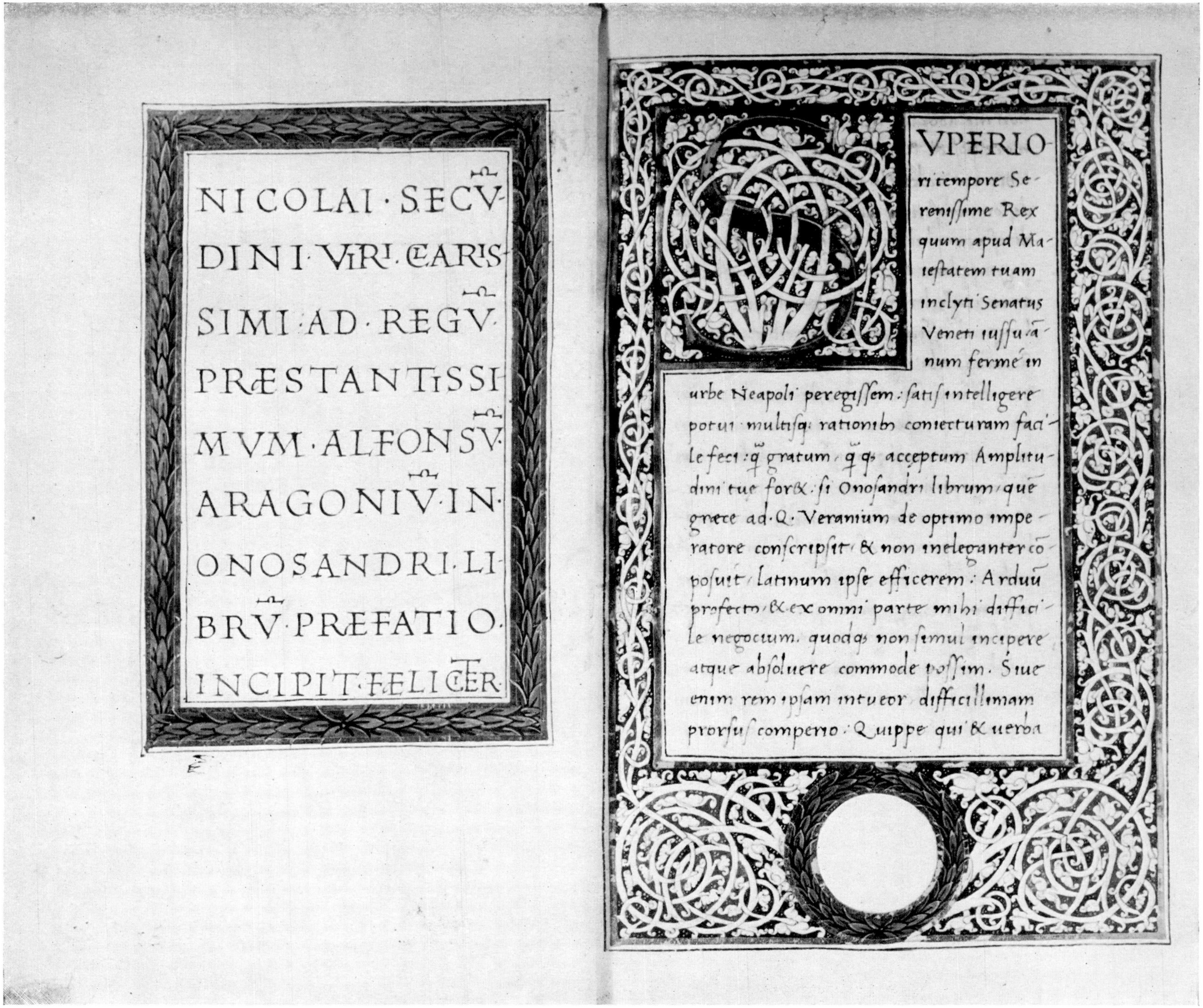

5. From *Onosander: De Optimo Imperatore.* Writing by Hippolytus of Luna. 1494

Petri Carmeliani Brixiensis poetę Suasoria
Letię ad angliam pro sublatis bellis ci
uilibus et Arthuro priñpe nato epistola

Nglia post tatas clades tatasq ruinas
Et tot cognata prelia facta manu
Post odium antiquum geminę de sanguie regu
Stirpis et innumeras gentis utriq neces
Te superum rector tandem prospexit ab alto
Cum facies esset tam miseranda tibi
Vndiq ciuili cum sanguine terra maderet
Inq tuis populis Luctus ubiq foret
Cum genitrix natum natus fleretq paretes
Et fratrem frater nupta pudica uirum
Filius et patrem fratrem quandoq necaret
Frater ... furens iret in omne nefas

6. From *Petrus Carmelianus: Laus Angliae.* Writing by the author. 1486

cunctasq; orchadas i occidentali oceano: ad aglonez inq;
eode: fortunatas isulas: ad Austz: parti vsu: parti assiduo
comeantiu testimoio no aliter pene: quaz ipaz italiam
aut gallias noscerem circuspicere: minariiq; cepim aliq
toq; scrupulosius iqrere sicubi udis emergeret: celebra
ta hæc oiuz lris isula. quaz i nro oceano & antiqx loca
uit auctoritas: & nc etia orietaliu pploz ac totius orbis
cfirmat opimio. Quid miria: euenit hiuic: qd sæpe clais
viris accidit. vt ubiq; sint quaz i patria notiores. pcon
tare occidetis accolas idocti ipm isule nom ignorant:
lris vtiq; claz nom isule e. Insula xo no min ignota:
quaz vulgo. Mihi quidez de hac re cu Ricardo quon
daz angloz regis cancellario fmo no ociosus fuit: Uiro
ardetis in genii n braz iscio. & qt i Britania gemitus:
atq; educatus: abditazq; rex ab adoscetia supra fidem
curiosus talib; prestim questiuculis enodadis aptissimus
videret. Ille aut seu ga sic sparet: seu quia puderet igno
rantiaz fateri (qui mos hodie miltoz e: q no intelligut: qua
ta modestia laus sit: hoi nato n nosse oia valeti: pfiteri
ingenue se nescire quod nesciat) seu forte (qd no suspicor
quia hui mihi archani noticiaz i videret. Rcndit certe
se dubietati meæ satisfactuz. sed no prius qua ad libros
suos quoz nemo copiosior fuit: i patriaz reuertisset (Erat
eim duz i amiticiaz eius icidi tractadis dni sui negotiis:
apd sede aplicaz pegrinus. ea scilicet tepestate: qua mt
prefatuz dominuz suu & fracoz Rege prima diuturni
belli semina pullulabat: quæ cruetaz messez postea ptuler.

7. From *Petrarch: Epistles*. Anonymous scribe. 1497

Tiberius retulit ad Senatu̅ vt inter cætera sacra recipe-
rentur. Ve᷑ cu̅ ex consulto pa̅t᷑ Christianos elimi-
nari vrbe placuiss̅̅&. Tiberius p edic̅tu̅ accusatoribus co-
minatus est morte. Scribit Tertulianus in Apologetico.
Multi Senato᷑ & Equitum Ro. interfec̅ti.

Tiberius in Campania moritu᷑.

Olympias. CCIIII.

ROMANORVM·IIII· C·CALLIGVLA ANN·III MENS·X·

I.	C. Cæsar cognomento Calligula Agrippam vinculis liberatum Regem Iudææ facit.	XXIIII. Iudæo᷑
	C. Semetipsum in Deos Transfert.	Agrippa
	Flaccus Luuius Præfec̅tus Aegypti multis Iudæos calamitatibus premit consentiente Alexandrino populo. & crebris aduersus eum clamoribus perso-nante: Synagogas quoq; eo᷑ imaginibus: statuis: aris, & uic̅timis polluit. Refert Phylo in eo libro: qui Flaccus inscribitur: hæc om̅ia se præsente gesta: ob quæ & legatione ad Caium ipse susceperit.	Ann·VII.
II.	Passienus filius ob fraude̅ hæreditatis suæ necatur.	I.
III.	Caius Memmi Reguli uxore̅ duxit impellens eum vt vxoris suæ patre̅ esse se scriber&.	II.
	Pontius Pilatus in multas incidens calamitates propria se manu interfecit. Scribunt Romano᷑ historici.	
	Caius Petronio Præfec̅to Syriæ præcepit vt Hieroso-lymis statuã suã sub no̅i̅e Iouis Maximi poner&.	
	Toto orbe Romano sicut Phylo scribit & Iosephus in Synagogis Iudæo᷑ statuæ & imagines, & aræ C. Cæsaris consecratæ.	

8. From *Eusebius: Chronica*. Writing by Bartolomeo Sanvito

EST ETIAM CIR
PERSCRIBVN
DAS VEL PAVCIO
RIBVS LITTERIS
NOTANDAS STV
DIVM NECESSARIVM. QVOD
partim pro uoluntate cuiusq. fit: partim usu
publico. & obseruatione communi. Nanque
apud ueteres qvum usus notax nullus ess&
scribendi facultatem maxime in Senatu qvi
aderant scribendo vt celeriter comprehenderent
qvaedam uerba atque nomina ex communi
consensu primis litteris notabant: & singulae
litterae qvid significabant in promptu erant:
quod in pronominibus: legibus publicis: Pon
tificumq. monumentis: iurisq. ciuilis libris &
nunc manet. Ad quas nationes publicas acce
dit etiam studiosox voluntas vt unusquisq.
familiares sibi cognitas pro uoluntate signa
ret: qvas comprehendere infinitum est. Pu
blice sane tenendae sunt qvae in monumen
tis plurimis & historiax libris sacrisq. pu
blicis reperiuntur. vt

A   Aulus.
AVG.   Augustus vel Augur.

9. From *Inscriptiones Antiquae*. Writing by Bartolomeo Sanvito. 1500

Quel che a tal cura cū lingegno anhela
Reuolga ben la disciplina et larte
Oue lastutia militar si cela.
Ihorrido inculto, et sanguinēte Marte
Da le delicie morbide ciuile
Come dalbergo indegno se diparte.
Versa cum gente di feruor hostile
Che indurita a laratro a Sole et uento
Si colca in terra et pasce il cibo uile.
Di tal sobole nacque lo incremento
Di Roma gloriosa madre antica
Che fu del mundo militar spauento
Corpi robusti nati a la fatica
Sono da congregar sotto la norma
Che dura pouerta tien per amica.
Questa e la prima disciplina e forma
Chel tyricinio electo si conoschi
Come dal bracco le perdice a lorma.
Locchio uiuace chel sopor non foschi
Il capo erecto impecturito et largo
Negli humeri, come huō ch tronca e boschi

.a.
Innocentius .iij.
de elec̄ .c.
venerabilem .

.b.
Gelasius pp .xv.
q̄ .vi. c. alius .

c
de senten. et re
in .c. y. li. vi .

in suis scriptis ostendit q̄ aurum non tam
pretiosius sit plumbo q̄ regia potestate sit
altior ordo sacerdotalis . Stephanus q̄q̄:
papa secundus Romanum imperium
in personam magnifici Caroli a Grecis
transtulit in Germanos . Alius ite Ro
manus Pontifex Zacharias scilicet
Regem Francorum non tam pro suis ini
quitatibus. q̄ pro eo quod tantę potestati
erat inutilis a regno deposuit : et Pipi
num Caroli magni imperatoris patrem
in eius locum substituit : omnesq̄: Fran
cigenas a iuramento fidelitatis absoluit .
Innocentius papa quartus Fridericum
Imperatorem suis ligatum peccatis &

126

11. From *Hadrianus: De Romanae Ecclesiae potestate*. Anonymous scribe. *c.* 1490

Ill.mo et Ex.mo S.re mio. El M.co Ambassatore Ferrarese mi ha dicto la ex.tia vra essere restata
contenta chel si facia lre de gratia ad vno m/ Bartholomeo di vecheti genoese
scolare, quale foe de quelli tredici scolari quali foreno banditi, et quali erano
quelli per quello referirno Mons.re da latruada et m/ Branda da castiono mandati
da la ex.tia vra a pauia per reformare ei studio che metteuano in confussione epso
studio, et perche alhora la ex.tia vra ordinoe de non fare gratia ad alcuno depsi scolari
perche pareua che caduno de loro quale fosse admesso in quello studio fosse sufficiente
a disordenarlo, et tirarlo a confusione, per questo mi e parso prima che io sy venuto
ad effecto alcuno de queste lre fare intendere alla ex.tia vra quanto ho dicto de sopra.
quale potera mo per sue lre significarme quello vole che circa questo facia: alla qle
ex. cordie me ricomando. Mli die 16 Junij 1498

Seruitor Bartholomaus chalcus

12. A letter written by Bartholomaeus Chalcus. 1498

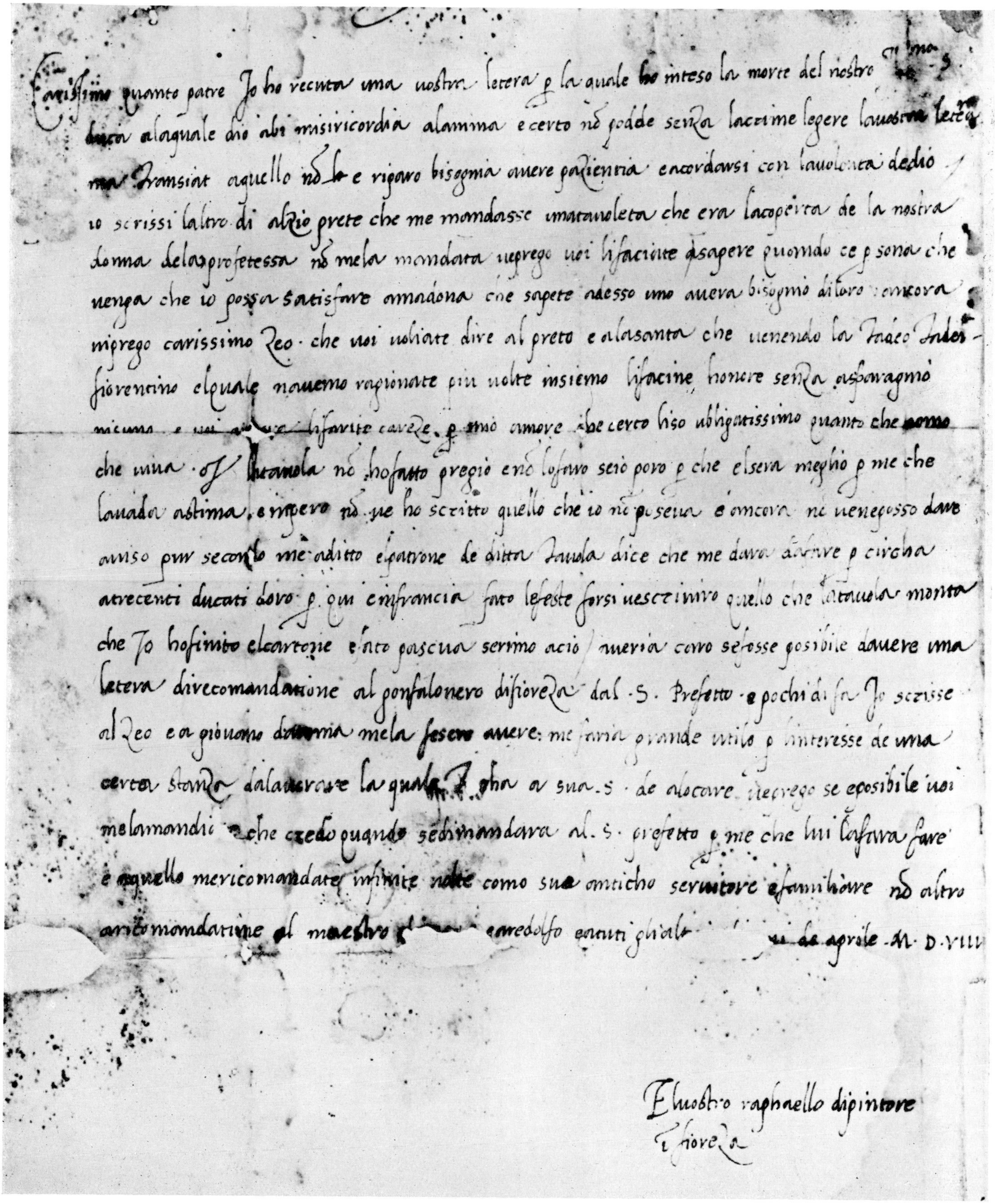

Carissimo quanto patre Io ho receuta una uostra letera p la quale ho inteso la morte del nostro Ill.mo S.
duca alaquale dio abi misiricordia alanima e certo nō podde senza lacrime legere la uostra letera
ma transiat aquello nō le e riparo bisogna auere pazientia eacordarsi con la uolonta dedio
io scrissi laltro di al zio prete che me mandasse una tauoleta che era lacoperta de la nostra
donna dela profetessa nō mela mandata uiprego uoi li facite asapere quando ce p sona che
uenga che io possa satisfare amadona che sapete adesso uno auera bisognio di loro ancora
uiprego carissimo Zeo che uoi uoliate dire al preto e ala santa che uenendo la Tadeo Tadei
fiorentino elquale nauemo ragionate piu uolte insiemo li facine honore senza asparagnio
nicuno e uoi ancora li farite carezze p mio amore che certo li so ubligatissimo quanto che omo
che uiua. P la tauola nō ho fatto pregio e nō lo faro se io poro p che el sera meglio p me che
la uada astima e impero nō ue ho scritto quello che io nō poseua e ancora nō ue ne posso dare
auiso pur secondo me a ditto el patrone de ditta tauola dice che me dara da fare p circha
a trecenti ducati doro p qui e in francia. fato le feste forsi ue scriuiro quello che la tauola monta
che Io ho finito el cartone e fato pascua serimo acio. auria caro se fosse posibile dauere una
letera di recomandatione al gonfalonero di fiorenza dal S. Prefetto e pochi di fa Io scrisse
al Zeo e a giouanno da roma mela fesero auere. me faria grande utile p linteresse de una
certa stanza dalauorare la quale tocha a sua S. de alocare. ue prego se e posibile uoi
mela mandiate che credo quando se chi mandara al S. prefetto p me che lui la fara fare
e aquello me ricomandate infinite uolte como suo anticho seruitore e famigliare nō altro
aricomandatime al maestro [illegible] e a redolfo e a tutti gli altri [illegible] de aprile M.D.VIII

El uostro raphaello dipintore
i fiorenza

13. A letter written by Raphael. 1508

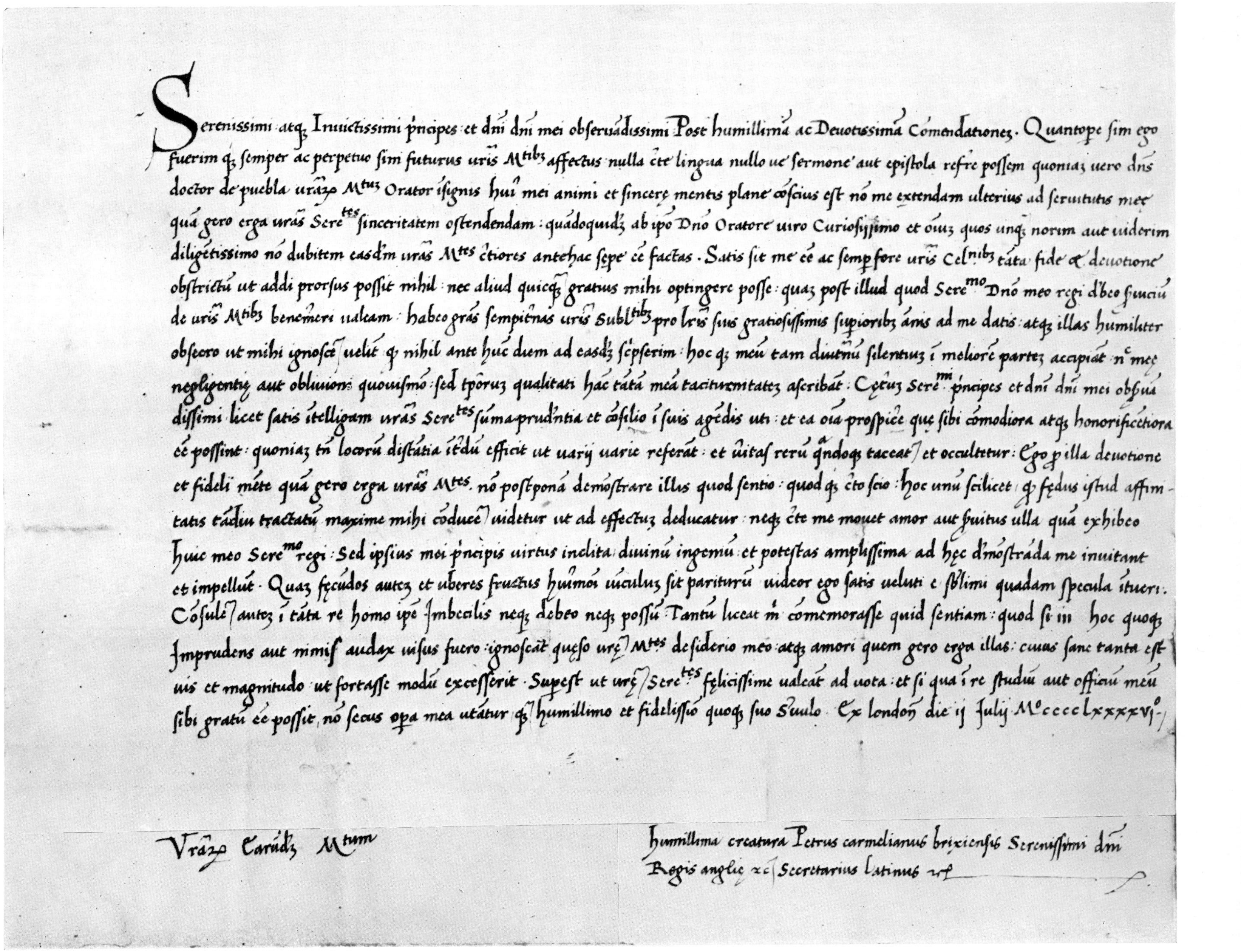

Serenissimi atq; Inuictissimi p̃ncipes et dñi dñi mei obseruãdissimi Post humillimã ac Deuotissimã Comendationez. Quantope sim ego
fuerim q; semper ac perpetuo sim futurus urĩs Mtibz affectus nulla ẽẽ lingua nullo ue sermone aut epistola refrẽ possem quoniaz uero dñs
doctor de puebla urãzo Mtus Orator isignis hui⁹ mei animi et sincere mentis plane cõscius est nõ me extendam ulterius ad seruitutis mee
quã gero erga urãs Seretes sinceritatem ostendendam: quãdoquidz ab ipõ Dñõ Oratore uiro Curiosissimo et oĩuz quos unq; norim aut uiderim
diligẽtissimo nõ dubitem easdẽm urãs Mtes ẽtiores antehac sepe ẽẽ factas. Satis sit me ẽẽ ac semp fore urĩs Celnibz tãtã fide & deuotione
obstrictũ ut addi prorsus possit nihil: nec aliud quicq; gratius mihi optingere posse: quaz post illud quod Seremo Dñõ meo regi d̃beo fnciũ
de urĩs Mtibz benemeri ualeam: habeo grãs sempitnas urĩs Subltibz pro lrĩs suis gratiosissimis supioribz ãnis ad me datis: atq; illas humiliter
obsecro ut mihi ignoscẽ uelit q; nihil ante huc diem ad easdz scpserim: hoc q; meũ tam diutnũ silentiuz i meliorẽ partez accipiat nc mee
negligentie aut obliuioni quouismõ: sed tporuz qualitati hac tãtã meã taciturnitatez ascribat. Cẽtuz Seremi p̃ncipes et dñi dñi mei obsuã
dissimi licet satis itelligam urãs Seretes sũma prudñtia et cõsilio i suis agẽdis uti: et ea oĩa prospicẽ que sibi cõmodiora atq; honorificẽtiora
ẽẽ possint: quoniaz tñ locorũ distãtia itdũ efficit ut uarij uarie referãt: et ũitas rerũ q̃ndoq; taceat et occultetur: Ego p illa deuotione
et fideli mẽte quã gero erga urãs Mtes nõ postponã demostrare illis quod sentio: quod q; ẽto scio: hoc unũ scilicet q; fedus istud affini-
tatis tãdiu tractatũ maxime mihi cõducẽ uidetur ut ad effectuz deducatur: neq; ẽte me mouet amor aut fuitus ulla quã exhibeo
huic meo Seremo regi: Sed ipsius mei p̃ncipis uirtus inclita diuinũ ingeniũ et potestas amplissima ad hec d̃mostrãda me inuitant
et impellũt. Quaz fecũdos autez et uberes fructus huiõi uiculuz sit pariturũ uideor ego satis ueluti e sblimi quadam specula ĩtueri.
Cõsulẽ autez i tãtã re homo ipẽ imbecilis neq; debeo neq; possũ. Tantũ liceat m̃ cõmemorasse quid sentiam: quod si in hoc quoq;
imprudens aut nimis audax uisus fuero: ignoscãt queso urẽ Mtes desiderio meo atq; amori quem gero erga illas: cuius sane tanta est
uis et magnitudo ut fortasse modũ excesserit. Supest ut urẽ Seretes felicissime ualeãt ad uota: et si quã i re studiũ aut officiũ meũ
sibi gratũ ẽẽ possit, nõ secus opa mea utãtur q; humillimo et fidelissĩo quoq; suo Suulo. Ex london die ij July Mo cccc lxxxxvj°.

Vrãzo Caritz Mtum

humillima creatura Petrus carmelianus brixiensis Serenissimi dñi
Regis anglie &c Secretarius latinus &c

14. A letter written by Petrus Carmelianus. 2 July 1496

H[enricus] Dei Gra[tia] Rex Anglie, et Francie, ac D[omi]n[u]s Hibernie. Ill[ustrissi]mo ac Ex[cellentissi]mo Principi D[omi]no Franc[isco]

And: Ammonius.

15. A letter from Henry VIII to the Marquis of Mantua. Writing by Andreas Ammonius. 24 June 1515

Dilecte fili noster salutê et apticam benedictionê. Mandauimus vener. fratri siluestro epis
ad Circuspectionê tuam quędam nostro nomine perscriberet: hortamur eam in domine
sub anulo piscatoris die xxvij augusti. M.D.XIX. Pont

16, 17. Papal briefs to Cardinal Wolsey. Writing attribut

Dilecte fili nr salutê et apticam bn. Amamus paterne dilectum filiu Petru corsum mercatorem flor
familia nobis aliqua secundum carnê affinitate coniuncta natus semper nos nostrãq domum
si se in patrocinio et familiaritate circuspectiois tua receptu viderit: ex causis praedictis tanq vi
rentes, ut illi in omnibus rebus et negociys suis: vbi fauore, gratia et auctoritate tua opu
Hoc.n. si fur ille idem petrus iã sibi persuasum habet, et nos de tua erga nos et hãc sancta
tuãq beniuoletia dignu cognoris, et nobis gratissimu feceris. Dat Rome Apud s. petru sub anulo pisca

1023
Vol.3

X

vincorniensi istius clarissimi Regis apud nos oratori prelato nostro domestico: ut
eius literis fidem indubitatam habere velis. Dat' Rome apud sanctum petrum
nostri   anno   Septimo

Ja sadoletus.

71   42

Ludovico Arrighi. 27 August 1519 and 15 October 1520

PP. X.

qui in Civitate londre negociatur cum propter eius industria et probitate, tum et q ex honesta
studio et affectu cum suis omnibus coluit et observauit. Hunc aute, qui sibi magno usui fore sperat,
nobis coniunctis et caris ei impense comendamus, ipsa Circ. tua hortantes in dno et enixius requi-
t (quod tamen honest et ex tua dignitate fiat) adesse et patrocinari nostra conplatione velis,
propesa voluntate et observantia in dno plene confidimus, benigne prestiturus, hoiem grani et modestu
e xv. octobr M.D.XX. Rom.   nri   anno   Octauo

Ja sadoletus

106   125

...a Regia Maie: humill comen · Cum mihi cognitum, et exploratu

sit, qua pietate, qua affectione, et amore olym Se: me: Sere[us] Pr

tuus Patruum meum Car[le] Senen: postea Pium .iij. prosequutus

sit, et quantis eum immortalibus benefitijs affecerit: uisum est mihi

Seren: Tuæ significare .S. D.N.D. Leonem X. hodie me in sacru

R[morem].D. Car[lium]: Collegium aggregasse · Quam dignitate mihi imeri

to credditæ aptica pietate: cupiens Patrem uestigijs inherere: illi si

gnifico, no minus ad obsequia, grataq3 seruitia Maie: Tuæ[tis] m

elitiq3 regni tui, ac tuorum omniu, q̃ ad ornamentum persone mece:

usumq3 Senen: Patrie Futura · Quare S. Maie: Tua[tis] rogo, atq3

obnixe obstero ut me Seruitore suu, ac reliquias Pij .iij. ample

cti dignetur: et opera mea ubi opus erit uti dignetur. inueni

et nepote (a) patruo no degenerare · Foelix Valeat .S. M. Tua[tas]

cui me ex animo Comendo: Ex vrbe Die iij Julij M.D.xvij

d[e] S[acra]: .Ma[tis]: Tuæ

Seruut. Jo: Car[his] Senē:

18. A letter from the Archbishop of Siena to Henry VIII. Secretary's hand. 3 July 1517

R^{mo} in Christo Patri et Dño Dño Thomæ diuina prouidetia Tituli Sanctę Ceciliæ Presby-
tero Cardmali, Archiepo Eboracensi, Aphcæ sedis Legato, Anglie Prmati et Cancellario: Thõs
Linacrus Medicus debitam obseruantiam

Quas proxime lucubrationes meas Clarissimo Regi nro dedicam, eor̃ R^{me} Pater exeplu nuc ad tē
mitto. Quo tuæ quoqz sanitati pro mrili secudu illius consulam. id quod optimo iure me facere ex
istimo, cu tu eius traquillitati, securitatiqz ita consulis ne (quod indignissimu alioqui sit, curæ
ullæ sanitatē eius possint couellere. Vtmagz ipse per imensas occupationes tuas, lucubrationes has
posses perlegere. Inuenires (nisi me nimiu amor operis fallit) quod nomihil ex Stomacho tuo eet.
Qui pro singulari eruditoe tua, no protmus quidlibet, sed tantu quod solida mmimit, admittis.
Hic aute nihil est gratis (ut aiut) dictu. Sed oia, partim certa methodo nmieta, partim fir-
missimis rationibus sic asserta, ut mille circiter et trecetis annis (tot enim sunt ex quo uixit author
nihil à quoqz in his sit refutatu. Sed siue tu eas releges, acerrimoqz iudicio tuo perpendes,
siue is qui pro tua sanitate tueda noctes diesqz uigilare pro officio debet: facile deprehedi
ex ipsis poterit, quibus rebus utens. quibusqz abstinens, no tutissimus modo à morbis, sed
etiam senectutē tua longissime differas. Cu interim nec illud opereprecui esse non possit:
cp ex his commentariis, priscoru quoqz mctus omnis ratio mtelligetur. Quæ si
cui cui mmus fortasse probabitur, quod uidelicet à nostra non nihil dissi-
det: is mennuisse debebit, eorum hanc Calculo fuisse com-
probatam, quorum hactenus sapientiam m omni
reliqua uite parte nuq satis miramur.
Quo magis hanc nostram po-
tius suspecta habere de-
cet, propterea cp
ab illa tme
aliena.
Va
le

19. Thomas Linacre. Dedication of a book to Wolsey. 1517

R̄me Dn̄e Dn̄e mi colendiss. humill. com̄en

...cause mouerint S.D.N. ut me ad Regem chr̄mū Ducesq̄ Cæsariani exercitus mitteret
cum ex R̄do Dn̄o Melchiore Langgo audiuit D. V. R̄ma scribere nil necesse est neq̄
ut obstinatis utrinq̄ atq̄ ad bellum inclinatis animis, nullæ quæ a S.S. proponerentur pacis conditiones sint auditæ scio etiam Dn̄i V. R̄mæ ita perspectam esse
et cognitum Beatnis S. erga se atq̄ Inuictissimum istum Regem beneuolentia, ut pro
certo habere possit quicuq̄ eo missus esset id imprimis habuisse in mandatis, ut
omnibus locis parem Stis S, sermi Regis ac D. V. R̄mæ dignitatis atq̄ amplitudinis conseruandæ curam gereret quod quidem cũ iussu S.D.N. tum nõ minus
etiam mea priuata animi propensione pro uris immortalibus beneficijs, a me diligetissime factum est, sed iucundissimum mihi fuit perspexisse eos qui inter se
pernitioso bello contendunt cæteris omnibus in rebus discordes mirabiliter consentire in opinione quam habent Inuictiss Regis ac D. V. R̄mæ uirtutis atq̄
prudentiæ quæ tanta est, ut etiam ijs quibuscum bellum gesserit sit admirabilis.
Mea uero missione quauis nihil ad spem concordiæ profectum sit tame in eo satisfactum est Smo D. N. qd omnes esse uoluit optimi animi sui testes, cum ut bonus
pater monendo rogandoq̄ nihil sibi reliquũ fecerit quod ad pacem tranquillitatemq̄ attinet chr̄næ reip̄cæ. Quod mihi D. V. R̄ma tam amater grās agit pro
nõ nullis meis in se officijs est id eius humanitatis: mihi quidem tot eius beneficijs obligato nihil potest esse iucundius q̄ ei seruire testariq̄ nõ ingratum
animum Meq̄ Dn̄i V. R̄mæ q̄ humill possum comendo Romæ xij
Decembris M D xxiiij

R̄mæ
D V

Humillimus seruulus,
Io: Matthæus El Veron.

21. A letter from Pasqual Spinula to Cardinal Wolsey. Secretary's hand.
6 August 1528

Henricus R

R(everendi) in X(ris)to p(at)r(es) & oratores n(ost)ri nob(is) q(ua)m plurimu(m) dilecti salut(em)/
Accepimus l(itte)ras v(est)ras et communes et p(ri)uatas dat(as) Rome xvij
Septembris) vltimo eiusdem mensis/ in quib(us) significatis l(itte)ras
n(ost)ras tam per Gronu(m) q(uam) alium Franciscum cursorem missas/ ad
manus v(est)ras saluas peruenisse/ tum etiam vos iuxta p(re)scrip-
ta a nobis mandata/ cu(m) pon(tifice) modis omnib(us) egisse/ vt quod
cupimus et petimus obtineatis ab eodem/ Qua in re etsi
operam studium et industriam v(est)ram adhibuistis/ tamen
apud pon(tificem) nihil promouere cam(?) nostram potuistis/ vt scri-
bitis/ sed frustra tentatis omnibus/ post traditas l(itte)ras nobili-
um/ aliquamdiu dum pon(tifex) consulere secum decreuerat/ de-
sistendum duxistis/ vt ad nos interim scriberetis/ Et reg(n)i
quidem n(ost)ri consuetudinem allegare distulistis etiamsi bono a-
nimo et n(ost)ro quidem iudicio poptime(?) fact(um) videatur: Nos
tamen maluissemus vos pretermisso consilio in ea parte minim(e)
me desiderato/ consuetudinem allegasse q(ua)m eam reticuisse/ atq(ue)
adeo vobis ut consuetudinem reg(n)i ac priuilegia allegetis
omnino mandamus/ Nam consuetudo et priuilegium reg(n)i/ ne
Angli extra Angliam litigare cogantur/ q(u)u(m) eiusmodi sint
q(uae) firmis/ et solidis rationib(us) subsistant ac nera(?) et iusta fun-

22. A part of a letter from Henry VIII. Secretary's hand. 7 October 1530

Risu continuo paris suaue, et
Circum dulciculos ferens ocellos,
Atque Annā digito nitente monstras,
En vobis, ait, vndecuq; summam,
Et dignam, aurea vel trecenta mala,
Vrtutū merito bono suarum
Que iam debeat hinc referre victrix.
Annæ haud hoc ~~munus~~ leue munus offerendū est,
Illam sceptra manent, manet corona,
Vrtutū preciū decens suarū .
Vos quicunq; decetis huc petitum
Formæ præmia inßerat venire,
Vobis insidias Dec parabat,
Et persundier haud leui rubore,
Cum vos ~~mitteret~~ huc tonas, volebat .
Tu pomū cape Cypri, vos q; Diue
Iam nūc ad superos polos redite .

Carmē Lelā Multi Dardamum mihi fuisse
di de indicio Dixerant Paridem elegantiore
Paridis. Formarum, simul et decoris ommis
Spectatorem, ageret greges per altam
Cum pastor mūeos superbus Idam,
Et malum daret aureum ter e qua
Aureæ Veneri manu, Minerua
Indignantibus, ac Iouis sorore,
Donec pulchra super uenret Anna.
Hec mecum reputans frequenter, nllo
Prorsus non potui modo nidere,
Quo mysteria tenderent stupenda,
Cum tu diua Venus, polo relapsa
Cursu ad equoreos cito Britannos,
Magnis dotibus underung clare,
Annæ cedis, et aureum lubenter
Das pomum sua dona pulchriori,
Cuius tam lepidum caput decore
Mox cinget rutilans corona gemmis.

23. A page of *Verses and Dities made at the Coronation of Queen Anne* by Nicholas Udall and John Leland. 1533

Pleas yt youre grace to bee aduertised that at thys tyme J do write vnto the same not only to make a
demonstracon off thys my procedinge in writinge, but also in my right humble and lowly wise to beseche youre
grace off youre dayly blissynge and pardone, for that J haue soo longe tyme delayed and forborne to write
vnto youre grace, to whos fauoure and goodnes no Creature liuing ys more bounde there J am, And like as
it hathe pleased almightie god and the kinges highnes moche pte by the meanes and good fauoure off youre
grace to preferre and aduance me in honor, So shal J (god willinge) endeuor my selffe and applie my
tyme for thattaynyng and encreas off lernynge vertue and cunnyng corespondente to the same, wherby
J may be more able to do vnto the kinges highnes suche seruice hereafter as shal consiste with his moost
gracous pleasure, wiche off all thyng vnder god, is and shalbe my oonly myende entent and purpoos
As maister Magnus thys berer Director off my Counsaill shall make Relacon vnto youre grace;
Whome almightie god euermore haue in his moost hoolie and blissed tuycon and gouernance, at Shiref
button the fourthe daye off Marche by youre moost humble Godsone

h. Rychemond

24. A letter written by Henry Fitzroy, Duke of Richmond, at the age of seven. 1526

4

Richardo Coxo

Quemadmodum officium meum postulat scribo
ad te literas Eleemosynarie charissime ut scias
me tui meminisse. Si enim non scriberem ad te
esset signu me tui obliuisci, sed nunc cum scri
bam ad te, est signu me te amare et tui memi
nisse. Et quemadmodum qui scribit ad unum
non potest non meminisse illius, quia scribit
illius nomen in superscriptione, sic ego cum
scribo ad te non possum obliuisci tui. Preterea
hortor te ut literae sint eque dulces tibi ac vena
tio et aucupiu delectant alios. Literae enim
sunt meliores thesauris. Et quicumiq tenet lite
ras, tenet magnu thesaurum. Nam dicitur
in paradoxis Ciceronis. Quod solus sapiens
dines, literae enim sunt diuitie. Saluta queso
Secretariu Regis, ac illi gratias age p pixidi
cula arenaria. Nunc optime vale mi elecmo
synarie ornatissime ac amantissime. Deus ne
sinat pedem tuam auerti a iusta uia. Hart
fordiae nono aprilis anno 1546.

Tui amantissimus discipulus
E. Princeps.

25. A page of a book in the handwriting of Prince Edward (Edward VI)

Sed quemadmodum ante dixi, non ita
adeo negligendę hę sunt concertationes.
Qui v̄ in tabernis ludi hodie fiunt illi me
maxime excruciant, et impietatis atq; in
temperantię multę plenę sunt: impietatis
quidem quod qui hoc faciunt dies observat
et augurijs addicuntur, et putant si noui
summm mensis huius cum voluptate et lę
titia degant, reliquum se annum sic trans
acturos: intemperantię v̄, q̃ cum prima
luce foeminę et viri pocula implentes, mul
ta cum intemperantia vinum merum hau
riunt. Non audis Paulum dicentem, dies
observatis et menses et tempora et annos
metuo vobis, ne frustra in vobis labora
uerim. Nempe extremę hoc est amentię
propter unum diem si auspicatus fuerit
per universum hoc expectare annum.

Hęc quanqũ vo, ip̃i non tacitę,
indigna tamen n̄ra religione
sunt, si vel alios hoc facere per
mittatis sine hij famuli vri,
sine Amici seu vicini fuerint.

26. A page of *S. Johanni Chrysostomi Homiliae.* Writing by John Cheke. 1543

yo.r graces singular fauor towardes me, hath alwaies been one of mi thefe confortes,
in mi diliget Service of y.e K. M. Which was y.e easier to me, bicause it was wel
taken. And althoughe in this defert of other mens troble, and mishap of mine
owne, I preciseli know not of yo.r graces fauorable goodnes towarde me, yet I
iudge y.t yo.r g. good minde towarde me, vndeferved to bee gotten, and vndeferved
to be loft again is sich, y.t I paffe the quietlier thorough the hole courfe of mi
damager, and fele y.e leffe storme of caufeles hap, bicause I do nuthe ftai miself,
in yo.r g. wifedome of taking thinges truli, and in yo.r goodnes of helping
the honeft fauorablier. Wherfore prefuming to give yo.r g. thankes for miself,
bicause I truft wel, and moost humbli requiring yo.r g. of continuais of yo.r
fauor worthilie as I truft to be beftowd on me, I ran not chufe but make
half a fute for half miself, being differtertd as yet from y.e other half of miself.
In mi wifes misbehavior towarde yo.r g. whosoever is forie for it I am moost forie,
not redie to excufe y.t which is fautie, but desiring of pardon, wherr forgivenes is
plentiful, and knowing y.t forgivenes of faues past, is amendment of time to
come, and no vice in ani mean woman bee so to great, but y.e vertue of nobilitee is
as large to merrir. Mi moost humble requeft therefor is, y.t yo.r g. gentilnes overcum
mi wifes faues, to fauor of clemencie, wherr iuftice wold have ftraitnes, to be
more noble in vertue then other be in offenfe, y.t wherr as faute is greateft, yo.r g.
mai moost appeare. In other matters I have charaged her to be plaine, and
I truft her honeft nature wil content yo.r g. Wheerin if she be fautie, I must
nedes naturalli pitie her, iuftli I ran not fpeke for her, and yet as I truft sche
wil shew herself true and plaine, so I wold faine fpeke if I thought ther werr
nede, and put yo.r g. in minde, y.t yow of wifedome consider y.t in yougth ther mai be
pardon, wheer experiens larketh, and towarde sich women pitie, as wifedome ran not
be loked for of, and towarde womn with chilse fauor for the inorentes fake.
But what meane I to enter into sich matters as yo.r g. knoweth best, and tel yo.r g.
y.t of yo.rfelf ye consider. Onli I beferhe yo.r g. and that moost humblie, to extende yo.r
grarious fauor so far above the requirers defert, as towarde mi wife and me both
as mi good minde towarde yo.r g. which is equal with yo.r greateft clientes, is above
mine habilitee, which is vndernrth y.e comen ftate of wel minded. God fend
yo.r grace moost ofperous eftate and long quietnes to his mightie wil.
From Westmester y.e XXViij of Januarie. 1549. 2 Ed. 6.

yo.r g. moost bownden
Orator Ioan Cheke

27. A letter written by John Cheke. 1549

Quod tanto temporis intervallo tam raras a me literas acceperis, Rex Illustriss.
quibus vel gratias agerem pro beneficiis, vel saltem debitam meam erga te
observantiam testatam facerem, spero facile me veniam impetraturam:
presertim cum nulla admissa sit cessatio oblivione quadam tui, cuius nunquam
oblivisci vel possum, vel debeo. Nunc vero cum tuam Maiestatem
in locis non procul Londino sitis versari intelligam, rumpendum mihi silentium
esse duxi, ut testificarer neque de debito meo erga te cultu quicquam esse
remissum, neque tua incolumitate quicquam mihi esse posse optabilius, quam
firmam & integram esse ex quorundam sermone cognovi. Ego sane
dum singula Dei Optimi Maximi beneficia mente recolo, hoc unum ex
omnibus maximum fuisse iudico, quod te Londini ex proximo morbo tam
subito & clementer restituit. In quem quidem te dei quadam providentia
lapsum esse arbitror, quemadmodum proximis literis ad tuam Maiestatem
scripsi, ut omni morborum materia pulsa, tu huiusce regni habenis tracta=
dis quamdiutissime servareris. Nihil ~~~~~~~ eque incertum aut minus
diuturnum quam vita hominis, nimirum qui & Pindari testimonio nihil
sit aliud, quam umbrae somnium. Et homine, ut ait Homerus, nihil terra
alit fragilius. Cum itaque cuiusque hominis vita tot tantisque casibus no[n]
modo sit exposita, sed etiam vincatur, singulari quadam divinae provide[n]=
tiae clementia et morbum preteritum abs te depulsu, & in istis locor[um]
(quos a morbis non plane immunes fuisse cognovi) & aeris mutationib[us]
tam crebris ab omnibus omnium morbor[um] periculis te servatu esse iudicamus.
Cui providentiae Maiestatis tuae tutelam committo, simulq[ue] rogo ut eandem
quamdiutiss: incolume servet. Ashridiae 20 Septembris

Maiestatis tuae humillima soror.
Elizabeta

Cum multa Sint Nobilissima, ac Amantissima Domina, Quæ me facile Inuitant hoc tempore
Ad scribendum nihil tamen Perinde me Mouet, atque Cura Valetudinis tuæ, quam ut Spero
Esse optimam, Ita de eadem Certiorem fieri Magnopere Cupio. Quare mitto hunc nuncium
Quem iudico fore tibi gratissimu, tum Propter artem illam Musicet, qua te Simul mecum
cupido oblectari non ignoro, tum quod a me, Profectus tibi certissime referre possit de omni
Statu, ac Valetudine mea. Atque sanè in animo fuit ante hunc diem, Iter ad te fecisse,
teque coram salutasse, uerum uoluntati meæ non omnia Responderunt: nunc spero hac
Hÿeme idque Propediem Propius nos esse congressuras. Quo sanè nihil mihi erit
iucundium magis, Aut magis uolupe. Cum autem (ut accepi) Summa Iam manus
Iimposita sit Per Maletum operi Erasmico in Iohannem (quod ad tralationem
Spectat) neque quicquam nunc restet nisi iusta quædam uigilantia, ac cura adhibeatur
In eodem corrigendo, Te obsecro ut opus hoc Pulcherimum, atq Utilissimum, iam
Emendatum Per Maletum aut aliquem tuorum Ad me transmitti cures, Quo suo
tempore Prelo Dari, Possit, atque porrò significes, an sub tuo nomine in lucem felicissime
Exire uelis, aut potius incerto authore: Cui operi mea sanè opinione iniuriam facere
Videberis, si tui nominis Autoritate etiam Posteris comendatum Iri recusaueris:
In quo, Acuratiss. transferendo tantos labores summo Reipub Bono suscepisti; Plures
(ut satis notum est) Susceptura, si ualetudo corporis Permisisset. Cum ergo
in hac re abs te laboriose admodum sudatum fuisse nemo non intelligat, cur quam
omnes Tibi merito deferant laudem reijcias non uideo, Attamen ego hanc rem omnem
Ita Relinquo Prudentiæ tuæ, Vt quamcumq uelis rationem inire eam ego maxime
Aprobandam censuero. Pro crumena Quam ad me dono misisti ingenteis tibi gratias
Ago. Deum opt Max precor ut uera ac incotaminata felicitate perpetuo te Beare
dignetur, in quo etiam diutiss ualeas. Ex hanworthia 20 Septembris

Tuæ studiosissima ac Amantissima

Katherina Regina

29. A letter written by Katharine Parr. 1544

EDWARDVS dei gratia Angliæ, Franciæ, et Hyberniæ Rex: fidei defensor: et ecclesiæ Anglicanæ, Hyberniaæq; supremum in terris caput. tiſſ. omnibus, et singulis ad quos presentes peruenerint salutem. Cū cum nō obscure ad nos relatum fuerit, Vicecomitem Bellacium ciuem Carentinū sub nostris militiæ præfectis ante hac stipendia meruiſſe et in ea rē fidelem, et strenuam operam nauaſſe preſentes cū litteras et testimonii, quod, sicut debet, plurimi facit non grauatim indulsimus, ut sicubi fortaſſe opus fuerit, eidem non desit hæc nostra opere ipsius, quam fideliter nobis impendevat, commendatio. teſ. Datum Londini ex Regia nostra Westmonasterij die xxvij mensis, Nouembris M.D.L. Anno uero regni nostrj Quarto

E Somerset
W. Wiltshire
W. Northt̃

F N Bedford Wyngfield Ve Nhi̋t

F A Darcy̋

SIGISMVNDVS AVGVSTVS DEI gratia Rex Poloniæ:
magnus Dux Lituaniæ. Russiæ. Prussiæ, Mazouiæ etcğ dominus et hæres. SEREn͂mæ
Principi Dominæ Mariæ eadem gratia Angliæ, Franciæ, etcğ Reginæ et Dominæ Hiberniæ etcğ.
Sorori et consanguineæ nostræ charissimæ Salutem et fælicium successuum continuum incrementum.
SEREn͂ma princeps soror et consanguinea nostra Charissima. Dedimus id negocij Mag͂co Alberto
Criski, Præfecto Dobrzinensi et ad Mtem vestram oratori nostro vt Mtem vestram viseret. atque
illi quædam nomine nos͂tro referret. Quapropter postulamus a Mte vestra vt et benignè illum
audiat. et dicenti fidem habeat. Quod nos pari vicissim studio Mti vestræ referre studebimus
cuius amori nos commendamus. eamğ bene valere cupimus. Dat͂ varsouiæ 19. Aprilis.
Anno domini M.D.L.V. Regni nostri XXVI.

bonus frater

Sigismundus Augustus
Rex sr̃.

... our heyghnes to vnderstande that y cause of my not
... to the same at francis last departynge from hens
... my beynge at the campe wythout vnderstandynge of the
... worde of hys beynge here. but sythens hauinge occatione
cum to my lorde ambasateur, and fyndynge a conveniet
messenger, I thought yt my bouden dutye to declare vnto
your Ma of the iernye the frenche kinge hath made
sythens hys returne out of almaynge. After our cuminge
into the duchye of lusenburge we passed by a smalle
castelle called rodemache, whether the kinge sent to haue
had vitaylle, comaundynge them as also to yelde but they
refusede both. Opon whyche occation there were the same
night 10 peces of ordynauce planted a gaynste hyt,
and the next morninge after they had beten hyt an
houre or more, the capitayne began to parle yeldynge
hymselfe to the kinges plesure, but to late for the
frenche men beynge gredye of spoyle and seynge sum
avauntage entred and slue all wythyne sauinge the
capitayne hys wyfe and hys 2 doughters. Ther
was feu found wythyne hyt at the same tyme
other then pesauntes, for the spaniardes coueyed
them selues auuaye the nyght before to a verye
stronge place called tweynville a leage of, and
4 leages from meats, whyche we affyrme to be
so stronge as the kinge wyll not medelle wyth
hyt. From thys castell he marched touwards astene
as I wrote to your heyghnes in my last letters y
he was determyned to do, but wythyne 2 dayes
the nuces was brought that hyt was yelded
to the Admiralle, so that the kinge chaunged
hys purpose

32. Part of a letter from Barnaby Fitzpatrick to Edward VI. 20 June 1552

æternam & futuræ uitæ felicitatem maximum. haberent momentum suggerere
quod ut tu mihi facere digneris cum neq ingenio nec eruditione nec pietate in=
fimus inter eos omnes haberi debeas iterum atq iterum a te peto. audacula
tibi uidear oportet quæ tam audacter hoc efflagito sed si consilij mei rationem
respicere uolueris nempe quod ex pietatis tuæ penu ea depromere cupiam quæ
cum ad mores formandos tum ad fidem in Christo Seruatore meo confir=
mandam conducere queant hoc quod facio mihi uitio uertere nec pro tua
humanitate poteris nec pro tua prudentia Volueris. Ex libello illo uera &
non fucata religionis pleno quem nuper ad patrem & me misisti tanquam
ex horto amænissimo flores suauissimos quotidie colligo & pater etiam dum per
grauissima negotia licet in eius lectione sedulo uersatur quem autem inde uteraq
importabimus fructum de eo tibi & deo propter te immortales gratias agere debemus
non enim æquum esse putamus ut per te tuiq similes quos non paucos hac in
parte felicissima parit Germania a Deo optimo Maximo tot tantaq uere di=
uina dona ingratis accipiamus animis. Solemus enim homines hominibus
ut par est beneficijs beneficia compensare & donorum collatorum memores.
nos præstare quanto magis igitur operam nauare debemus diuinæ boni=
tati si non ex omni parte respondere at saltem lætis animis quæ confert am=
plecti & ex animo pro illis gratias agere. Nunc ad laudes quas mihi tribuit
tuæ literæ uenio quas ut nec uendicare ita nullo modo agnoscere debeo sed
quicquid mihi diuina bonitas largita est id omne acceptum illi refero tan=
quam mearum rerum omnium quæ uirtutis aliquam speciem habent au=
thori summo & eum quem meo nomine roges uelim Ornatissime uir assiduis
tuis precibus ut me hac in parte measq rationes omnes ita moderetur ut
tanta eius benignitate non indigna reperiar. In animum induxerat Illu=
strissimus pater meus ad Tuam Humanitatem scribere pariterq gratias
agere pro tuis præclare susceptis laboribus & singulari illa humanitate qua
inductus es suo nomine Quintam Dec. inscribere eiusq auspicijs in lucem
ædere nisi grauissimis Regiæ Maiestatis negotijs in ultimos Britanniæ fines
fuisset auocatus sed ubi per publicas occupationes uacabit quam diligentis=
sime ad te scribere se uelle affirmat. Postremo hebraicari iam incipienti
mihi si uiam & modum aliquem ostenderis qem in hoc studiorum
cursu tenere maxima cum utilitate debeam me longe tibi deuinctissimam
reddideris. Vale totius Ecclesiæ Christianæ summum Decus & ornamen=
tum & te diu nobis suæq Ecclesiæ superstitem seruet Deus Optimus
Maximus.   Tuæ pietati Deditissima
                           Iwanna Graia.

in primisque placare contendam.
Idem censuit & sanctissimus
illud vas dei Paulus, quo cum a
Christo discesseris, nihil maius
aut sublimius habes, cum dixerit
totius legis impletionem mutua
quandam et coniunctam essedi-
lectionem.
Hy ergo qui distractis ais
et voluntatibus in dies singulos
rixis, et contentionibus studet
praetergquam quod universas
dei leges perfringunt atque dio,
fant, hanc ipsam etiam omnem
praeclaram rerum fabricam qua
tum illi maxime possunt convel.

Expositiones quaedam an
tiquae in Epistolam
Divi Pauli ad Phi
lemonem ex
diversis
Sanctorum Patrum
graece scriptis com
mentarys opera &
diligentia Oecumeny
collectae et nunc
primum la
tine ver
sae.

Cantabrigiae Anno dni 1542.

a.1

34. Pages of *Expositiones quaedam Antiquae in Epistolam Divi Pauli ad Philemonem*. Writing by Roger Ascham. 1542

SANCTISSIMO Patri, ac Dno nro, D. MARCELLO II°, diuina Prouidentia Pontifici Max°. Philippus et Maria, Dei gratia
Rex et Regina, Angliæ, Franciæ, Neapolis, Hierusalem, et Hiberniæ. Fidei defensores atq̃ Cum Ecclesia Metropolitana
Eboracen. iam vacet, Pastorisq̃ solatio destituta sit, Rdmum in Cho Prem, D. Nicolaum Hethe, fidelem nrm Consiliarium, v. Sti
commendamus: Qui antea etiam a nobis, v. Stis feliciss. Predecessori, commendatus est. Huius viri, singularis doctrina,
probitas, vsusq̃ rerum suffis et constantia facit, vt singulari eum iam assiduo prosequuti simus amore, et precipua nunc etiam
in eo commendando vtamur ratione. Hic ad Ecclesiam (vt ipsa ferebant tempora) vocatus, prium Roffen. deinde
vigorinen., vtramq̃ sane in omni superiorum temporum motu, quiete prudenterq̃ gubernauit. Postea, cum in vestra
Catholicæ Disciplinæ via insistere, q̃ in errores abduci maluerit, spreta omni et fortunarum amissione, et capitis etiam dis-
crimine, in carceris aū passus est ftagm., à v. S. tc petimus, vt Ecclesiæ Eboracen. iam vacanti, de
Persona predicti Rdi pris Nic. Hethe prouidere dignetur illi in Archiepm Pastoremq̃ preficere, et curam atq̃ administra-
tionem ipsius Ecclesiæ sibi plenarie committere. v. Stos dignetur. DEVS v. S. conseruet et tueatur. Ex Regia nostra
Hamptoniæ, Quarto Maij

v.ræ Stis

Do   L°   M.

Humillimi Filij

[signatures]

Maria

35. A letter from Philip and Mary to Pope Marcellus II. Writing attributed to Roger Ascham. 1555

t per ch'era cortese & n'hauea forse Non men de duo augurj il petto caldo
a Spada trasse, e minacciando corse Doue poco di lui temea Rinaldo
auito che potea tutto li porse Pur come l'elmo hauesse arato & baldo
in volte s'eran gia non pur ueduti M a al parragon dell'arme conosciuti
ominciar quiui una crudel battaglia Come a pie si trouar coi brandi ignudi

Bennardino Cataneo Scriuea al
Signor Odoardo Ralyg
Gentilhuomo In
glese

36. From a specimen book written by Bernardino Cataneo. 1545

...amente ho io scritta questa sorte di lettera cosi grande per
che nella grandezza de corpi, et delle aste si possa conoscere
l'arte, et la misura dello scriuere, perche ne i caratteri
piccoli non ui si possano cosi bene scorgere come in questi
si fanno; ha si adunque a formare il corpo da un quadro
bislongo d'onde la maggior parte delle lettere si formano:

37. From a specimen book written by Petruccio Ubaldini. 1550

P che e troppo molesta

al cor che dolce sia

la gratia c'altrui fa preda e prigione

m'è libertà pa questa

tuo somma cortesia

più che du furto altiero amor soppone

di par passi e ragione

ma se lu da più che l'altro no dorra

e be giusta quistione

che lu sormonta e l'altro nol p dona

fra ghamici e quistione

risposto dilo

5

38. A madrigal written by Michael Angelo

Eccellentissimo et molto mio osseruandissimo M. Michelagnolo

Per ch'io nõ credo, ch mai altromo nascessi al mondo, piu affetionato alle gran'virtu vre di quello, et sono stato io, comiciãdo a cognoscerle quando io lauorauo della bella oreficeria et p esser in uaghito di quelle vre uniche uirtu, nõ mi pareua d'hauer satisfato alla honesta uoglia mia, se prima io nõ ueniuo conesso alla mirabile scultura, p sempre amandouj, et osseruandouj io mi son fatto qualche honore et tutto di pende da uoi.

Hora considerato che gli homini ueramẽte sono obligati s ad amare, et osseruar l'uno l'altro: trouandomj io adunque em mio lauorate, il quale p le grã bta sua mi son fatto compare, et uedutolo uolto, p alcunj suo comodi, auenirsene in cotesta bella roma; ancora saputo da luj et altre uolte egli ui ha seruito in nel farre certi capitelli p la grã fabbrica di S. Pietro: doue io son certissimo p esser luj homo ualete nel arte, et hij ui debbe essere riuscito: p la prego, et p amor mio uoi ui degniate di metterlo Topa ch'io nene terro molta obligatione: Egomandouj sempre ch mi comãdiate: Et Iddio felicissimo lungamẽte mi conserui. Di Fize il di 3 di settembre 1561 sempre parauissimo alli comandi uostri

Benuenuto Cellini

39. A letter to Michael Angelo written by Benvenuto Cellini. 3 September 1561

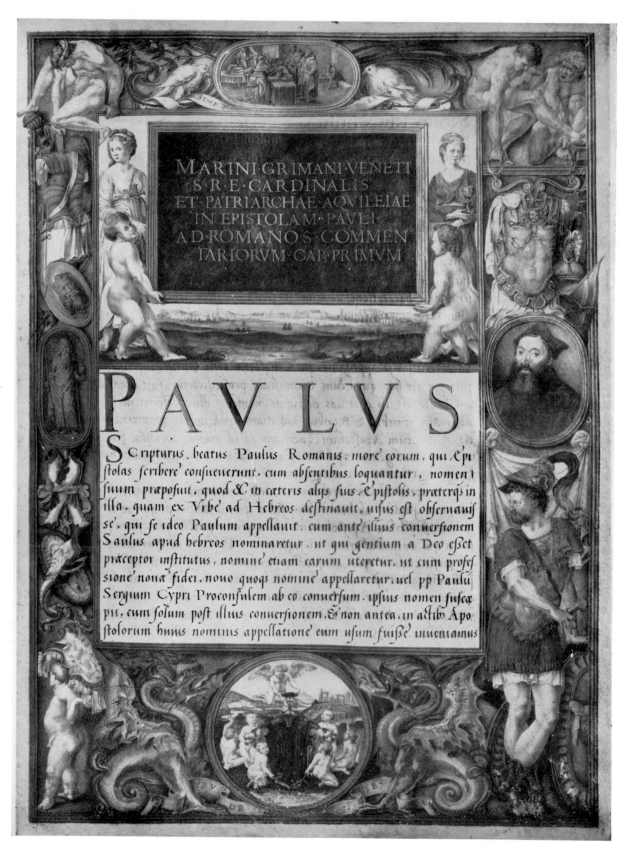

MARINI·GRIMANI·VENETI
S·R·E·CARDINALIS
ET·PATRIARCHAE·AQVILEIAE
IN·EPISTOLAM·PAVLI
AD·ROMANOS·COMMEN
TARIORVM·CAP·PRIMVM

PAVLVS

Scripturus, beatus Paulus Romanis, more eorum, qui Epistolas scribere consueuerunt, cum absentibus loquantur, nomen suum præposuit, quod & in cæteris alijs suis Epistolis, præterqs in illa, quam ex Vrbe ad Hebreos destinauit, uisus est obseruauisse, qui se ideo Paulum appellauit, cum ante illius conuersionem Saulus apud hebreos nominaretur, ut qui gentium à Deo esset præceptor institutus, nomine etiam earum uteretur, ut cum professione noua fidei, nouo quoqs nomine appellaretur, uel pp Paulū Sergium Cypri Proconsulem ab eo conuersum, ipsius nomen suscæpit, cum solum post illius conuersionem, & non antea, in actibs Apostolorum huius nominis appellatione eum usum fuisse inueniamus

40. From Grimani's *Commentary on St. Paul's Epistle to the Romans*

Il Gastaldo veramente, che contrafacesse à quanto è ditto di so:
pra, sia immediate priuo de l'ufficio suo, et sia fatto in suo luoco.
Vlterius alli |25| Settembrio |1530| essendo sta preso in que-
sto Consiglio, che li Procuratori nostri de Citra douesseno nel
far delle eleemosine andar loro medemi per li Sestieri a dispe-
sar à poueri bisognosi. Però sia preso, che li detti Procuratori
che andaràno à far tal dispensation, non possino dar più d'un
ducato per vn alli poueri, et se trouasseno persone di tal sorte
miserabile, et vergognose, che li paresse per conscientia sua de
darli più, debbano tuor in nota cadaun de quelli, et in Procu-
ratia referir el tutto alli suoi Compagni, doue à bossoli, et bal-
lotte li possi esser di quella eleemosina, che alle conscientie loro
parerà delli danari deputati a ditte eleemosine :—

 Li Procuratori non possano mostrar el Tesoro ad alcuno
  senza parte presa nel Consiglio di .x. Cap. C. xlj:

D1534. Die. 29. Julij. In Consilio decem cū additione :—
Ouendosi conseruar la opinione, che è quasi in tutte
le parti del mondo delle zoie, et Tesoro, ch'è in el Santuario
della Chiesa nostra de San Marco, se diè principalmente
tuor via vna larghe za, et facilità, che hanno et huomini, et dō-
ne Terrieri, et forestieri di veder ditto Tesoro, el qual se die tener
con tutta quella reputatione sia possibile per honor del Stado

41. *Laws and Regulations to be observed by the Procurators of the Church of St. Mark of Venice.*
Writing by Presbyter Johannes de Vitalibus. 1558

Ó ueramente beati et felici quelli che se', & ogni sua cosa uolontariamente han posta ne le sue mani, et ne la sua podestà.

ℭ SOPRA IL TERZO SALMO
il qual fece David mentre
fuggiua da Absa-
lone' :~

Si lamenta del popolo suo, che si era ribelato ad Absalone suo figliuolo, et suo nemico; & poi con l'aiuto di Dio saldamente stabilisce' l'animo suo. Quando ci uiene addosso qualche' tribulatione rifuggiamo à questo hynno, quasi come à una rocca; et considerando ben questi uersi confirmiamo talmente l'animo, che non possa essere ismosso da la costanza, ne spinto à far cosa, che non stia bene à la dignità del christiano; il quale ne i dolori, ne' la istessa morte non dee' ne muouere, ne pie'gare, essendo massimamente breui et leggie're tutte le cose, che chiamiamo mali del corpo, et de la fortuna, benche muouano piu

42. From *La Paraphrasi* by Flaminio. *c.* 1545. Writing in the style of Ferdinando Ruano

humano hai superata et uinta; et quello
che maggiormente è da lodare in te, serua-
sti la uita a tutti li caualieri, et al Signor lo
ro, et conseruasti li cittadini di quella senza
offesa et di robba et di uita, segno certo de
grandissima integritade, et summa clementia et temperantia, et quello che piu impor-
ta in uno Principe, osseruatore de la fede, ne
ancora ti diletti, come molti Rè et Imperatori han fatto, di spargere il sangue humano, ma sempre perdoni a tutti quelli che 'l
furore de la guerra ha perdonato, con lo ini-
mico armato hai guerra, con li uinti perpetua pace. Impero non è marauiglia se
li dei ogni tua impresa fauoriscono. Ma
per tornare doue ho lassato, giudicando
TV cosa brutta stare in otio, un'altra uolta
intrasti con nuouo essercito nel regno de li
Vngari, et uenuto a battaglia con loro; su-
perasti lo essercito, et priuasti il Rè de la
uita et del regno con grandissima uittoria
subiugando quelli populi ferocissimi con
li quali tante uolte li tuoi antiqui hanno

43. From Panegyric to Suleiman the Magnificent. (Mid-16th century)

et violenti affin cò'il
giudicio de poueri nõ
sia transcurato et cò'
gloppressi sieno libera,,
ti et sopra tutto cò'la
religine fiorisca et ac,,
cresca et si come è tè
piaciuto d'ornare del
tuo santo nome i no,,
stri magistrati cosi
etiamdio ti preghiamo
si come tu sei buono cò
per loro opera et mini,,
sterio i fideli mentre

cò qui viuono ti ser,,
uino puramente &
viuino santa mente
si cò'in sieme cones,,
so loro a te peruenghi,,
no cò'sei il Re de
Re. et il Signore de
Signoreggianti oue
tutti insieme godino
delli eterni beni &
felicita per Giesu Chri,,
sto nostro Si,,
gnor &
Amen.

44. From Queen Elizabeth's Prayer Book. 1578

NAVIGATION DE LA MER AVEC LES HAVRES, RADDES, PROFONDITEZ,

DANGERS, ET APPROCHEMENS DES

costes, depuis le fleuue Humbre Nort: coustoyant alentour du

Royaulme d'Escoce tirant aux Isles Orchades, et Hebrides

iusques a la Mulle de Gallouuay, & la Riuiere de Soluay

Premieremet composée par Alexandre Lyndesay Escossoy,

soubz le commandement du Roy d'Escos se Jacques cinquiesme,

du nom, (&) depuis remise en son entier, auec

augmentation. et illustration de

plusieurs figures

&

descriptions tresnecessaires

pour la nauigation. Par Nicolas de

Nicolay, du Daulphine ;

Geographe du

Roy.

45. From *Navigation*. Writing attributed to Pierre Hamon. *c.* 1560

Omnem & obseruantiam debuit nobilissimis maioribus tuis, dum ~
uiuerent, Academia nostra (Illᵐᵃ Regina) & mortuis pro immumerabi-
libus in se benificijs gratam piamᵃᵍ recordationem quotidie præstat.
Earum ad tuam Maiestatem, uel illo nomine solo, permagna pars ia
antea redundauit: sed quo nouo exemplo, uel renouentur tota, quæ
fuerunt, uel singulari cum nominis splendore in Serenitate tua
augeantur, tua regia munificaᵍ liberalitate nuper effectum est.
Priuilegijs quibusdam & immunitatibus sic munierunt olim studia
nostra Progenitores tui, ut sata disciplina illa ingenua ac liberali,
fructum hunc quem cernimus communis hodie Resp. percipiat: sed
eorum aliqua, siue temporum quandoᵍ iniquitate interrupta, siue
quod uerisimile fuerit, nonnulla dissuetudine dimissa, ad uberiore
bonarum literarum spem, a tua Celsitudine non solum reuocata,
sed plane amplificata, ac confirmata sunt. Immortale sane beni-
ficium, & cuius eo magis laus omnium uoce, literis, prædicatione propterea celebranda sit, quod non tam a supplici nostra imploratione,
qua tamen moueri seᵍe gloriosum fuit, quam ab interiori quodam,
qui in regio tuo pectore latet, uirtutis doctrineᵍ sensu totum profectum esse uideatur. Quod nos quidem libentissime hoc tempore ag-
noscimus, gratiasᵍ Vsᵍ eo referre non desinemus, quoad et uel obᵍ-
uantiæ partibus, quæ sunt in nobis perquam sane exiles, uel uotis
quotidianis, quæ nostræ nationi communiter cum cæteris conceduntur,
aliqua ex parte satisfacere possumus. Huc addas licet uel uitam
ipsam, quam pro tua Maiestate profundere non dubitabimus: cuius
quidem iacturam in communi ac perpetua uita literis per te restitu-
ta parui momenti ducendam putamus. Nimis ista ambitiose colligere
nolumus: ne illa etiam opus est, in tam exquisita doctrina Serenita-
tis tuæ, quæ ad consequentium temporum subsidia & patrocinium
maiorem alioqui in modum contendenda essent. Tantum Maiestatis
tuæ diuinæ cuidam prudentiæ, cum alumnos bonarum disciplinarum
qui hodie uiuunt uniuersos, tum ipsam, quæ & istos, & reliquam pos-
teritatem continet, Academiam commendamus.   Dominus Iesus ~
Serenitatem tuam in omni uirtutis, fortunæᵍ splendore nobis Reiᵍsp
quam diutissime conseruet incolumem.   Cantabrigiæ
Pridie Nonas Maij   M. D. LXI   E Senatu nro.

Maiestatis tuæ Supplices
Procancellarius, & reliquus
cœtus Cantabrigiensis Senat.

46. A letter from Cambridge University. Writing attributed to
Bartholomew Dodington. 1561

...quòd, pro tua singulari in bonas literas beneuolentia, & præstanti item in Repub. vel authoritate, vel gratia, te sibi Patronum Academia nostra asciuit, Clarissime Vir: fit quidem vt hoc nomine Scholastici ad Honorem tuum, non solum coniunctim vniuersi, sed separatim etiam singuli impeditis rebus suis confugere non dubitent. Horum ex numero mihi vel infimo tenuissimoque aditus iam antea perfacilis tua humanitate patuit: illeq́ue quo in tempus omne posterú ac consequens munitior esset beneficentia tua effectum est, qua me totum in fidem tuam tum benignissimè suscepisti. Quò minùs dubitabo rem, quam suspicor quosdam ex nostratibus pro scriptis multoç interpositione amicoç apud Honorem tuum prosequuturos esse, solus pro meipso apertè simpliciterq́ue agere. Vacat iam, Clarissime Vir, obitu cuiusdam docti Viri Oratorium, vt vocant, in Academia munus. Eius ipsius competitores tres sumus, qui singuli magna quidem suffragioç spe mouemur, sed ita de exitu propter alienam a nostra ratione Electionis formam, dubitamus, vt nemini nostrú id munus Academiæ consensu obtingere posse putemus. Quid enim est in eius causa qui electus tum habendus sit, è tribus quibusq́ue eligentia præsentibus, duos ex præscriptione Statuti ire debere? Atq́ue formula quidem Comitioç huiusmodi nó alia nobis ex maioç instituto proponitur: qua sanè difficile erit cuiuis nostrû voto potiri, imprimisq́ue hoc tempore mihi, nisi (quæ facta est tibi post tertiam rogationem ex Statutis nostris potestas) tu me tua, diligenter totius negoty habita ratione, suffragatione adiuueris. Nihil ego hoc in loco ambitiosè: quin æquitate & prudentia tua singula modereris maiorem in modum vehementerq́ue rogo. Quod mihi, vtcunq́ue ceciderit, maximi instar beneficy erit, tuusq́ue me Honor ista ratione ad officiú illud, quod tibi, ex quo me ad te contuli imprimis debeo, nouo etia vinculo arctioris cuiusdam obseruantiæ astringes. Dominus Jesus Honorē tuú nobis, & reipub. quàm diutissimè conseruet incolumem. Cantabrigiæ

Idibus Octobris. M. D. LXI.

Honori tuo deditissimus
Bartholomæus Dodingtonus.

47. A letter written by Bartholomew Dodington. 1561

Collegii sanctæ et individuæ Trinitatis
in Cantabrigien. Academia fundator

HENRICVS

eius nominis Octauus Angliæ Fran. &c Rex, hoc Collegium, quod à
sancta et individua Trinitate nomen habere voluit, fundauit An° D 1547°
Anno regni sui vltimo

E Aulæ Regiæ quæ nunc dic to Trinitatis Collegio
Vnitur, fundator

EDWARDVS eius nominis tertius Angliæ Fran. Rex &c
Aulæ Regiæ iussu paterno fundator An° D 1337. Regni sui Vndecimo,
eius nepos Richardus 2 multa bona eidem Collegio contulit.

Domus Scholarium S. Michaelis, quæ item vnitur
Collegio Trinitatis, fundator

HERVICVS de S Tanton Clericus, Domus Scholarium S. Michael.
fundator. Anno D. 1343° An Regni Edwardi tertij decimo septimo.

Eiusdem Collegij Benefactores

MARIA Angliæ Franciæ &c Regina, annuo redditu hoc
Collegium auxit Anno D 1554. Anno Regni sui primo.

GVLIELMVS Filey sacræ Theologiæ professor et Somersama
in comitatu Huntingdon Rector. Anno D. 1549. Regni Edwardi sexti secundo.

LAVRENTIVS Moptit sacræ Theologiæ Bacchalaureus,
Collegij corporis Christi Magister Anno D. 1557° Annis Philippi et Mariæ
quinto et sexto.

HENRICVS Adams Eccliæ sancti Michaelis in Cantabrig
ædituus. Anno D. 1557. Annis Phylippi et Mariæ 5. et 6°

IOHANNES Christoferson Episcopus Cices treusis, quondam huius
Collegij socius, postea Magr. Anno Dni 1558. Anno Regni Elyzabethæ 1°

48. From a list of Benefactors and Scholars of Trinity College, Cambridge. 1563

REMONSTRATIO CHRISTIANA.

NEMINEM esse nostrum arbitror, Viri Religiosissimi, qui se cum videat inique ad necem usque impugnari, non assurgat in deffensionem sui, sentiens vero se viribus inferiorem non recurrat ad auxilium eorum, quos sibi fautores sperat, aut propter æquitatem causæ quam sustinet, aut propter furorem impugnantis, quem sedare expedit, ne calamitas in commune tandem redundet. Itaque Senatus Populusque Ruppellensis, reliquiæ miseræ & fragmina deploranda Ecclesiæ Christianæ quæ per Gallias dispersa est, cum se furiosis maximisque copijs obsessã, multis varijsque assultibus impugnari conspiceret, ad auxilium vnicum Omnipotentis confugit, de cuius fauore non dubitarunt, quod illius pariter de causa gloriaque agebatur. Proinde Deus ille exercituum ostendit se cordibus Regum Principumque dominari, & quicquid illis est vel rei vel virium, id sua vniuersum esse in manu positum, qui bellum cruentissimum admirabili pace commutauit. Porrò quia latebat miseros istius hora liberationis & Diuini subsidij, interea fuit huc recursus, ad eadem in causa iam olim afflictos, vnde munitiones bellicas, frumenta, aliaque ad vitæ sustentationem necessaria compararent, sine quibus subsistere non poterant in expectatione auxilij operisque Diuini, si illud longius vlteriusque deferri contigisset. Vbi plurimorum piorum huius Vrbis ciuium nunquã non satis laudanda erga illos spectata cognitaque est beneuolentia, qui necessitati suorum in Christo fratrum libenter suppeditarunt. Quod quidem beneficium illis tanti æstimatur, vt ne vel minimam eius partem recompensatione se posse consequi putent. Quamquam interea nihil magis optant, quam retribuendi facultatem dari: vnde sanè procul absunt in presentiarum. Tanta enim rerum conditionisque suæ facta est mutatio, vt vix se se ipsos intuentes recognoscant. Quippe de Vrbe munitissima mœnibusque circunsepta, de Vrbe celebri atque opulenti, cum terræ fertillitate, tum vario comerciorum genere, nauigationibusque externis, quid aspicere restat quam confusum destructione aceruum? Ædes partim demolitas ad exaggerationem mœnium, partim crebris hostilium balistarum ictibus deiectas; portum vadumque constipatum; Villas denique agros vineta, salinas passim deuastata, vt taceam æraria publica, fortunasque priuatas diuturna & superioris & istius belli grassatione exhaustas, adeo vt quo suam conditionem plus contemplantur, hoc miseriorem comperiunt. Attamen Deus dedit, Deus abstulit, & olim meliora dare potest. Ideoque facilius omnia tolleranda, si qua tranquillitate certa & continua frui contingat. Si non in expendia redeundum foret alia prioribus maiora, quibus integrum & tutum, vel sartum & tectum (vt aiunt) restituantur. Si non premantur aliunde postulatione obligationum, & ratione æris mutuati; Quæ tamen tria, licet grauissima, euitari nullo modo possunt. Nam si certum quod

Anti-

49. A remonstrance from the Senate and People of La Rochelle. 1573

Quod solent homines à Deo precari vt in ecclesia et in patria sua florenti et beata, pace pia atq̃ æterna fruantur id te
regnante (Illustrissima princeps) nos subditi tui consecuti sumus. Idq̃ maiestati tuæ (sicuti debemus) sancte
et cum omni pietate gratulamur. Quod quidem nos alumnos tuos quibus virgula diuina sceptri tui literarum
quietem et sapientes leges, iura, et priuilegia confirmasti, facit vt spem maiorem concipiamus ad hoc ipsum
quod in præsenti necessario facimus, sine omni metu certaq̃ cum spe aggrediendum, et vt in maiestatis tuæ
authoritate (quod facimus) tanquam in opportuno iustitiæ, iurisiurandi, et pietatis portu acquiescamus. Qua=
re amputata omni prafandi ratione rem ipsam breuissime expediemus. Accepimus nuperrime literas maiestatis tuæ, quarum hæc summa est: vt Antonium Wingfeld (socium collegij nostri) abiecta omni cuncta-
tione et sine villa mora ad Rectoriam quandam nostram de Caissharo in comitatu Bedfordia, vt collegij nostri firmarium admittamus, id quod nobis adhuc leges nostræ, et statuta non permittunt. Statuti enim nostri hæc verba sunt, vt nulla omnino reuersio (quam vocant) vllius rectoriæ, manerij, fundi, agri, aut
possessionis cuiuscunq̃ ad Collegium spectantis vnquam concedatur aut dimittatur, nisi biennio
ad summum ante terminum in singulis indenturis expressum, plene completum et finitum,
sub pæna periurij et locorum suorum in perpetuum amittendorum. Quod cum terminus in
priori dimissione nondum confectus et completus est excepto biennio vt requiritur, hæc rectoria adhuc in
nostram potestatem non venit vt in hoc ipso præsenti tempore nulla interposita mora illam denuo dimitta=
mus. Multa præterea graues rationes, et causæ iustæ afferri possunt, quibus adducimur, vt humiliter et
demisse omnes a maiestate tua precemur vt hoc totum (quicquid est) nobis permittatur, vt rectoria hæc,
similesq̃ alia (quoad commode fieri potest) sic elocentur, vt numerosa studiosorum multitudo, quæ quotidie
in hoc Collegio alitur inde aliquid accipiat, quod vt petamus lex nostra nos cogit quæ uibet, vt illa summa
quæ pro fine (vt vocant) commode sumi potest ad Collegij vsum conferatur. Sed nos pro officio et
obedientia nostra, nostra omnia vestræ serenissimæ maiestati (vt debemus) permittimus, et tuæ volunta-
atq̃ voci omnia subijciemus, vbi id te velle intellexerimus. Deus opt: max: Serenissimam maiestatem
tuam ecclesiæ et reipublicæ nostræ quàm diutissime seruet incolumem. Datum Cantabr. tertio Idus
Decembris 1579.

Maiestatis tuæ humillimi subditi

Joh: Still.
Iacobus Bill   Edw. Dolling
Guilielmus Farrand   Geo: Gronning
Robertus Thacker   Leonardj Chambors.

Richard woods   Anthonius Rudde.

50. A letter from Trinity College to Queen Elizabeth. 11 December 1579

Honoratissimè Domino, D.ᵈᵉ Burghley,
summo totius Angliæ Thesaurario,
et Acad: Cant: Cancellario
dignissimo εὐδαιμονᾶν

Qui grauius ære alieno premuntur, de nouo mutuum petere aliquid non audent, ne audiant illud, quod objici huiusmodi hominibus solet: Item prius quod debes solutum oportuit quàm de nouo quicquam incipias petere. Est quod ab Honore tuo petam (Honoratissimè Burgleiensis) est tamen quod tibi debui iam diu adeo vt pro veteri tua sane quàm eximia beneuolentia simul gratias agere, et nouam aucupari gratiam pudeat. Hæc tibi (quæ mihi nunquam ex animo excident) exciderunt, credo: quomodo aut ego tibi notus fuerim, aut tu mihi aliquid profueris aliquando. Dicam igitur pace tua, et breuiter vtrumq. Qui nunc sum Cantabrigiensis, olim Westmonasteriensis alumnus fui: vbi cùm essem, lectissima Domina vxor tua, mea qualicunq in transcribendis græcis quibusdam vti opera voluit. Vsa est idq non tum solum mihi fuit vtile, sed multo deinceps magis. Nam non multum post, inter Honorem tuum et Westmonasteriensis Collegij Decanum optimum et ornatissimum D.ᵉᵐ Goodmannum, habitus vltro citroq sermo est de discipulis ad vtramq Academiam eligendis. De nominibus puerorum quæritur. Nominor inter alios et ego. Petis, ecquid vt pulchrius scribebam quàm cæteri, ita cætera quoq responderent. Mitto alia, Te authore nominatur Palmer, qui Cantabrigiam eligatur. Eligor et iam versor Cantabrigiæ versariq diutius vellem: sed vereor ne sine te non possim. Primus tu mihi è viris Primarijs Princeps amicorum meorum omnium extitisti: primus et solus mittendi me ad Academiam author fuisti. Nunc peto, vt retineri in Academia, vt quem hactenus ornasti noui accessione honoris ornari magis, vt pristina tua conseruari beneficia velis. Non nisi suasu tuo Collegij Trinitatis discipulus sum factus, nunc eiusdem Collegij te suadente, et per gratiosas tuas literas intercedente fieri Socius discupio. Prius illud beneficium ne petenti quidem vltro erat delatum: hoc petenti & vehementer illud quidem, quæso vt deferas. Res quam peto, tam mihi erit grata, quàm quæ gratissima. spes vero quam propono admodum est incerta, nisi adiuuante me cum summa causæ æquitate, summa gratia et authoritate tua. Tua Amplitudo nisi adsit perierunt omnia mecum: sin adsit sic mihi spero euenturum vt volo: sic qui tibi viu quàm cæteris plura debui, debebo deinceps omnia. Deus te summum religionis et reip: præsidium, nostraq Academiæ patronum, diutissimè seruet incolumem.

Μοῖτε φίλοι μάλα, καὶ κάλλιςτερ ἐπὶ φρεσὶν ἴναι
Ἐ νεκ ἐμεο δοκεῖ τοῦτο οι διαεομενω·
Κ ου φιλοντε καλόντε τόδε κρηἴκον ἐλάδωρ,
Αυφοͅεͅοͅοι καλόν·μοι μιγͅα, ουι ὀλιγον.
Καὶδι ου με͂, ἀλλων ρα φίλων ἤτινα οἶδα·
Γωῖτος ιε͂ις ου φίλος, καὶ μοὶ Θͅ·ἴδι φίλ Θͅ·
Σ οι γᾳͅ ο ͂ καλον ἔςιν ἐνι ͅηδͅνᾳι φίλον κ͂ͅε·
Ἡ λίωφη κͅ μοι συ φίλι·ἔͅι μόνη.

Amplitudini tuæ
deuinctissimus

Ioannes Palmer
Cantabrigiensis

51. A letter from John Palmer to Lord Burghley. 2 September 1581

Most Gratious Soueraine Lady, The God of heauen and earth, Who hath mightilie, and evidently, given vnto your most excellent Royall Maiestie, this wunderfull Triumphant Victorie, against your mortall enemies) be allwaies, thanked, praysed, and glorified: And the same God Almightie, euermore direct and defend your most Royall Highnes from all evill and encumbrance: and finish and confirme in your most excellent Maiestie Royall, the blessings, long since, both decreed and offred: yea, euen into your most gratious Royall bosom, and Lap. Happy are they, that can perceyue, and so obey the pleasant call, of the mightie Ladie, OPPORTVNITIE. And, Therfore, finding our duetie concurrent With a most Secret beck, of the said Gratious Princess. Ladie OPPORTVNITIE, NOW to embrace, and enioye, your most excellent Royall Maiesties high favor, and gratious great Clemencie, of CALLING me, Mr Kelley, and our families, hoame, into your Brytish Earthly Paradise, and Monarchie incomparable: (and, that, abowt an yere since: by Master Customer Yong, his letters,) J. and myne, (by God his fauor and help, and after the most conuenient manner we can,) Will, from hencefurth, endeuour our selues, faithfully, loyally, carefully, warily, and diligently, to ryd and Vntangle our selues from hence: And, so, very devowtely, and Sowndlie, at your Sacred Maiesties feet, to offer our selues, and all, Wherein, we are, or may be hable, to serve God, and your most Excellent Royall Maiestie. The Lord of Hoasts, be our help, and Gwyde, therein: and graunt vnto your most excellent Royall Maiestie, the Incomparablest Triumphant Raigne, and Monarchie, that euer was, since Mans Creation. Amen.

Trebon. in the kingdome of Boemia, the 10th of Nouebre: A. Dni : 1588 : styl. vete.

Your Sacred and most excellent
Royall Maiesties :
most humble and dutyfull
Subiect, and Servant :
8 John D

52. A letter from John Dee to Queen Elizabeth. 10 November 1588

VIVAT SERENISSIMA ANGLIÆ REGINA,

Vestræ Maiestati Regiæ ab Illus-
tri Mauricio Orangiæ Principe, Comite de Nassau, Hol-
landiæ, Zeelandiæ, Occidentalis Pheisiæ, Ultraiecti et Transysula-
niæ prouinciæ Gubernatore Domino meo clementissimo, demisse et re-
uerenter admodum hasce offero Literas, in fauorem supplicis Libelli istis adiunctæ scriptas, cui Libello à capite ad calcem intente lecto,
si eadem Vestra Maiestas, vel octauam horulæ partem, à grauissimis
regiis negocys, benigne dignetur indulgere, intelliget perspicue, quanti
sit momenti, Regiam vestram personam, sanctissimumque pri-
uatum suum concilium, scire quæ eo continentur.
Quantum ad Libelli supplicem, Ideo quod ab vltimo vestræ
Maiestati oblato libello, eâdem Ma.te inscia, tam indigne
et contumeliose sit habitus, veritus ne nunc peius haberetur
non audet se patefacere. Verum ille licet extraneus et vestræ
Maiestati regiæ nulla religione et fide, sit deiunctus, tamen
regia vestra manu munitus, sese sistet, re ipsa docturus, pro
regia Vestra dignitate, magna alacritate, vel decies, se malle
mortem oppetere, quam sincere, Regiam vestram personam,
dictumque secretum concilium, id ignorare, quod Libellus
dictat. Quod reliquum est, ad integram foelicitatem
nihil mihi deerit, si incolumis hinc, et vestra Regia pace, hoc
est, sine vitæ periculo, hoc Ma.tis vestræ Regno, contingat
excedere, Dei beneficio, meo Principi totiq́ Patriæ, perpetuò
prædicaturus, tantam tanta Christianæ Principis humanitatem et beneuolentiam.

53. An enclosure to a letter from Captain Wybrandt Bornstra. 1590

Righte honorable and my very good Lorde my duty moste humbly reviembrede beinge,
beinge lothe to aquante your Lordeshippe with this my bade writynge but rather then
J wolde be condemnede to be vnmyndefull of my duty J rather chuse to be thoughte,
vnskillfull with most humble and dutyfull thankes for your Lo: manyfoulde cinnes,
ses every waye shouede daly towardes me and the greate care which your Lo: hath of,
me with my humble thankes that it dide please your Lordeshippe to give my Lorde,
Marquis thankes for me who husethe me very honorably and likewise my Ladye,
who J finde a very kinde and honorable Lady to her smale power. acknoledgcinge,
my selfe moste bounde to your Lordshippe for the moste parte of my chese hapines,
humbly craiinge your Lo: blessinge J humbly take my leave. prayinge for your,
Lo: longe life and muche hapines. Tidworth.

Your Lo: humble and omoste,
obedyente doughtere

Lucy St Johne

54. A letter from Lady Lucy St. John to her father, Lord Burghley. 1588

O god all-maker, keeper, and guider: Inurement of thy rare-seene, vnused and seeld-
heard-of goodnes, powred in so plentifull sort vpon vs full oft; breeds now this
boldnes, to craue with bowed knees, and heartes of humilitye thy large hande
of helpinge power, to assist with wonder oure iust cause, not founded on Prides-motion
nor begun on Malice-stock; But as thou best knowest, to whome nought is hid
grounded on iust defence from wronges, hate, and bloody desire of conquest. For scince
meanes thou hast imparted to saue that thou hast giuen, by enioyng such a people, as
scornes their bloodshed, where suretie ours is one : Fortifie (Heare God) such heartes
in such sort, as their best part may be worst, that to the truest part meant worst
with least losse to such a Nation, as despise their liues for their Cuntryes good.
That all Forreine Landes may laud and admire the Omnipotency of thy Worke:
a fact alone for thee only to performe. So shall thy name be spread for wonders wrought
and the faithfull encouraged, to repose in thy Vnfellowed grace : And wee that mynded
nought but right, inchained in thy bondes for perpetuall slauery, and liue and dye
the sacrificers of oure soules for such obtayned fauoure. Warrant, Deare Lorde
all this with thy command. Amen

55. A prayer said to have been written by Queen Elizabeth. 1597

My intention to attend your Highnesse to morrow (God willing) cannot stay me from acknowledging by these few lines how infinitely I am bound to your Highnesse for that your gratious disposition towards me which faileth not to show it selfe vpon euery occasion whither accidentall or begged by me, as this late high fauour and grace it hath pleased your Highnesse to do my kinsman at my humble suite. I trust to morrow to let your Highnesse vnderstand such motiues of that my presumptio as shall make it excusable. For your Highnesse shall perceiue I both vnderstand with what extraordinary respects suites are to be presented to your Highnesse; and withall that your goodnesse doth so temper your greatnesse as it encourageth both me and many others to hope that we may taste the fruites of the one by meanes of the other. The Almighty make your Highnesse euery way such as I, mr Newton, and Sr Dauid Murray the onely intercessours I haue vsed in my suites or will in any I shall present to your Highnesse wish you, and then shall you be euen such as you are, and your growth in vertu and grace with God and men shall be the onely alteration we will pray for. And so in all humility I Ceasse.   From London the 18 of October 1605

Your Highnesse

most humble and dutifull
Arbella Stuart.

56. A letter written by Lady Arabella Stuart. 1605

57. From *La Operina* by Ludovico Arrighi. 1522

Per seguire poi l'ordine de l'Alphabeto im=
parerai di fare questa linea I principia=
dola con lo primo tratto grosso et piano

dala quale ne cauerai le littere in=
frascritte

b d ff f b k l ſ ſſ ſf l bll lb ſl

& per fare che habbiano la ragione sua
li farai in cima quella te
stolina un poco piu groſſeta che la linea,
La qual grossezza tu facil=
mente farai

se facendo il primo tratto lo comen=
ci alla riuersa, & dapoi
ritorni indrieto per
lo medesmo

I b dff b kllllbbſſſl

58. From *La Operina* by Ludovico Arrighi. 1522

LITERA DA BREVI.

A a b c d e e f g g h i k l m n o p q r s s t u x y z

~: Marcus Antonius Casanoua :~

Pierij vates, laudem si opera ista merentur,
Praxiteli nostro carmina pauca date.
Non placet hoc; nostri pietas laudanda Coryti est;
Qui dicat hæc; nisi vos forsan utrạ monet;
Debetis saltem Dijs carmina, ni quoạ, et istis
Illa datis. iam nos mollia saxa sumus.

A A B B C C D D E E F F G G H H I I
K L L M M N N O P P Q Q R R S
S T T U V V X X Y Z & & & &

Ludouicus Vicentinus scribebat Romæ anno
salutis M DXXIII

59. From *Il Modo de temperare le penne* by Ludovico Arrighi. 1523

**HENRICO OCTAVO BRITANNIAE
GALLIAEQ REGI INVICTISSIMO
GAVFREDVS CHAMBER ·S·P·**

RE
VER
surus in Patri
am, idest i Re
gnum tuum .
Rex Inuictis
sime', illud me' præcipue diu solicitum
habuit, quidnam ex hac mea Italica
peregrinatione' Tibi afferrem, in quo
omnes cogitationes totumqs animum
meum semper in Maiestatem Tuã, ubi
cunqs gentium propensum testari pos
sem: Qua solicitudine leuari mihi uisus
sum quumprimum Apologi quidã Pan

dulphi Collenucy Pisaurensis uix antea
uisi ad manus meas peruenissent : Con
siderabam enim huiusinodi munere' po
tiori parti tui hoc est animo Tuo satis
factum iri posse', Vnde' ei non inutilis
delectatio afferretur . Quod fortasse
pluris facturus esses qǔ omnes Italicas ad
te comportatas opes : Quibus præsertim
ut omnibus fere reliquis bonis omnes
orbis terrarum Reges antecellis : Per
specta enim iam diu mihi est illa uere
Regia Indoles Tua, quæ' animi dotes,
corporis aut fortunæ' bonis anteferre'
solet . Habebis itaqs in Collenucy Apo
logis quod animum tuum abunde, tum
delectare', tum ad prudentiam prodesse'
possit : Fuit enim (ut fama est) uir

60. From *Collenuccio: Apologues*. Dedication to Henry VIII. Writing attributed to Arrighi

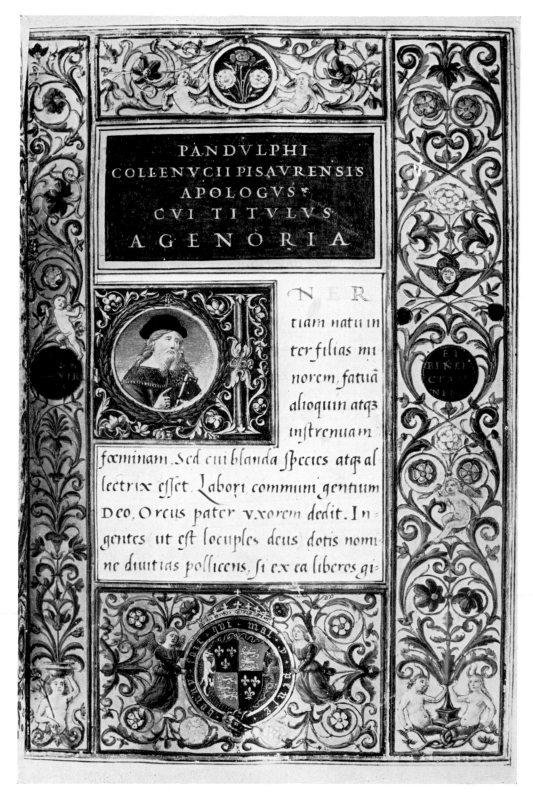

PANDVLPHI
COLLENVCII PISAVRENSIS
APOLOGVS·
CVI TITVLVS
AGENORIA

NER
tiam natu in
ter filias mi
norem, fatuã
alioquin atq̃
inftrenuam

fœminam, Sed cui blanda ſpecies atq̃ al
lectrix effet. Labori commum gentium
Deo, Orcus pater vxorem dedit. In
gentes ut eſt locuples deus dotis nomi
ne diuitias polliccns, ſi ex ea liberos gi

61. From *Collenuccio: Apologues*

62a. From a book of hours.
Writing attributed to Arrighi

62c. Arrighi's second type in the printed edition of *Sophonisba*. September 1524

62b. A fragment of *Sophonisba* manuscript.
Writing attributed to Arrighi

a b c d e f g d e gb k i l j m n o p q r s t u z v ç x ẓ y th pb ȝ ɓ.

A B C D E F G CH e GH K I L M N O P Q R S T U Z V Ȝ X Y TH PH H.

a ƀ ce de e effe ge e gbi kis i ille ji emme enne o pe qu erre se u esse te u zca vu ceta iese ese tbe phe baca.

e e e i o u u.

oi au ci iu ci ia ie io iu oi uo.

ab	ac	ad	af	ag	d	am	en	ep	ar	et.
eb	ec	ed	ef	eg	el	em	en	ep	er	et.
eb	ec	ed	ef	eg	el	em	en	ep	er	et.
ib	ic	id	if	ig	il	im	in	ip	ir	it.
ob	oc	od	of	og	ol	om	on	op	or	ot.
ob	oc	od	of	og	ol	om	on	op	or	ot.
ub	uc	ud	uf	ug	ul	um	un	up	ur	us	ut.

bra cbra dre fre gbre pre vri bro cbro pru tru sbra gri skia sla sma smo Ste Spron Sta Strin svo.

ba cbs ds fa gbos la ja ma na pa ra ss ta sa za va ça.
be cbe de fe ge gbe le je me ne pe re se te se ze ve çe.
be cbe de fe ge gbe le je me ne pe re se te se ze ve çe.
bi ci cbi di fi gi gbi ki ji mi ni pi ri si ti si zi vi çi.
bo cbo do fo gbo lo jo mo no po ro so to so zo vo ço.
bo cbo do fro gbos lo jo mo no po ro so to so zo vo ço.
bu cbu du fu gbu lu ju mu nu pu qua gue gui ru su tu su zu vu çu.

O Padre nostro, che in i cieli stai,
Laudato sia 'l tuo nome, e'l tuo valore;
Vegna ver noi la pace del tuo Regno.
In terra fatto sia lo tuo volere;
Come si fa ne la celeste corte.
Dà hoggi a noi la cottidiana manna.
E così come il mal, che havem sofferto,
Perdoniamo a ciascun, e tu perdona
Quel, che havem fatto contra i tuoi precetti.
Non ci tentar con l'antico aversaro;
Ma fa, che siamo liberi dal male.

       Amen.

A ve Maria di molte grazie piena,
Con teco sia l'altissimo Signore.
Tu fra le Donne benedetta sei;
E benedetto il frutto del tuo ventre
Iesu. O Madre de l'eterno Sire,
Porgi i tuoi dolci prieghi inanzi a suo
Per noi, che siama erranti, e peccatori.

       Amen.

C hi dirà queste in genocchi devoto,
Col volto volto verso l'oriente,
E col cappello giu del suo capello,
Speri, del voto suo non sarà voto.

63. Janiculo's typesheet of the second italic type of Arrighi. *c.* 1529

Anglici · Matrimonij.

Sententia diffinitiua

Lata per sanctissimum. Dñm Nostrum. D. Clementem. Papā. vij. in sacro Consistorio de
Reuerendissimorum Dominorum. S. R. E. Cardinalium consilio super validitate Ma
trimonij inter Serenissimos Henricum. VIII. ƺ Catherinam Anglie Reges contracti.

PRO.

Eadem Serenissima Catherina Angliæ Regina,

CONTRA.

Serenissimum Henricum. VIII. Angliæ Regem.

Clemens Papa.vij.

Hristi nomine inuocato in Trono iustitiæ pro tribunali sedentes, & solum Deum præ oculis habentes, Per hanc
nostram diffinitiuam sententiam quam de Venerabilium Fratrum nostrorum Sanctæ Ro. Ec. Car. Consistorialiter
coram nobis congregatorum Consilio, & assensu fecimus in his scriptis, pronunciamus, decernimus, & declaramus,
in causa, & causis ad nos, & Sedem Apostolicam per appellationem, per charissimam in christo filiam Ca
therinam Angliæ Reginam Illustrem a nostris, & Sedis Apostolicæ Legatis in Regno Angliæ deputatis interposi
tam legitime deuolutis, & aduocatis, inter prædictam Catherinam Reginam, & Charissimum in christo filium Henricum. VIII.
Angliæ Regem Illustrem, super validitate, & inualiditate matrimonij inter eosdem Reges contracti, & consumati rebusꝗ alijs in
actis, causæ & causarum huiusmodi latius deductis, & dilecto filio Paulo Capissucho causarum sacri palatij tunc decano & pro
pter ipsius Pauli absentiam Venerabili Fratri nostro Iacobo Simoneæ Episcopo Pisaurien. vnus ex dicti palatij causarum Auditori
bus locumtenenti, audiendis instruendis, & in Consistorio nostro Secreto referendis commissis, & per eos nobis, & eisdem Car
dinalibus Relatis, & mature discussis, coram nobis pendentibus, Matrimonium Inter prædictos Catherinam, & Henricum An
gliæ Reges contractum, & inde secuta quecunꝗ fuisse, & esse validum, & canonice validaꝗ, & Canonica, suosꝗ debitos de
buisse, & debere sortiri effectus, prolemꝗ exinde susceptam, & suscipiendam fuisse, & fore legitimam, & præfatum Henri
cum Angliæ Regem teneri, & obligatum fuisse, et fore ad cohabitandum cum dicta Catherina Regina eius legitima coniuge, illamꝗ
maritali affectione, & Regio honore tractandum, & eundem Henricum Angliæ Regem ad præmissa omnia, & singula cum
effectu adimplendum condemnandum omnibusꝗ iuris Remedijs cogendum, & compellendum fore, prout condemnamus, cogimus, &
compellimus, Molestationesꝗ, & denegationes Per eundem Henricum Regem eidem Catherinæ Reginæ super inualiditate, ac fœ
dere dicti Matrimonij quomodolibet factas, & præstitas fuisse, & esse illicitas, & iniustas, & eidem Henrico Regi super il
lis ac inualiditate matrimonij huiusmodi perpetuum Silentium imponendum fore, & imponimus, eundemꝗ Henricum Angliæ Re
gem in expensis in huiusmodi causa pro parte dictæ Catherinæ Reginæ coram nobis, & dictis omnibus legitime factis condem
nandum fore, & condemnamus, quarum expensarum taxationem nobis imposterum reseruamus.

Ita pronunciauimus ·I·

Lata fuit Romæ in Palatio Apostolico publice in Consistorio die. XXIII. Martij. M. D. XXXIIII.

Blosius.

64. A broadsheet showing the third italic type of Arrighi. 1534

65*a*. From a supplication written by G. A. Tagliente. 1491
65*b*. From *Lo presente libro insegna* by G. A. Tagliente. 1524

THESAVRO DE SCRIT TORI

Opera artificiosa laquale con grandissima arte, si per pratica come per geometria insegna a Scriuere diuerse sorte littere: cioe Cancellaresha: merchantesha: formata: Cursina: Antiqua: moderna: et bastarda, de piu sorte: cum uarij, e bellissimi exempli. & altre sorte littere de uarie lingue: cioe Grecha: hebraicha: Caldeu & Arabicha: Tutte extratte da diuersi et probatissimi Auttori: & massimamente dalo preclarissimo SIGISMVNDO fanto nobile ferrarese: mathematico: et Architettore eruditissimo: dele mesure, e ragione de littere prima inuentore: Intagliata per Ugo da Carpi: Cum gratia: et Priuilegio

A S

Anchora insegna de atemperare le Penne secundo diuerse sorte littere, e cognoscere la bontade de quelle, e carte, e fare iuchiostro et Verzino, Senaprio, e Vernice: cum multi altri secreti pertinenti alo Polito: et Eccellente Scrittore: come per te medesimo legendo imparerai. Ne lanno di nostra salute.

·M·D·XX·x·V

66. From *Thesavro de Scrittori* by Sigismundo Fanti. 1535

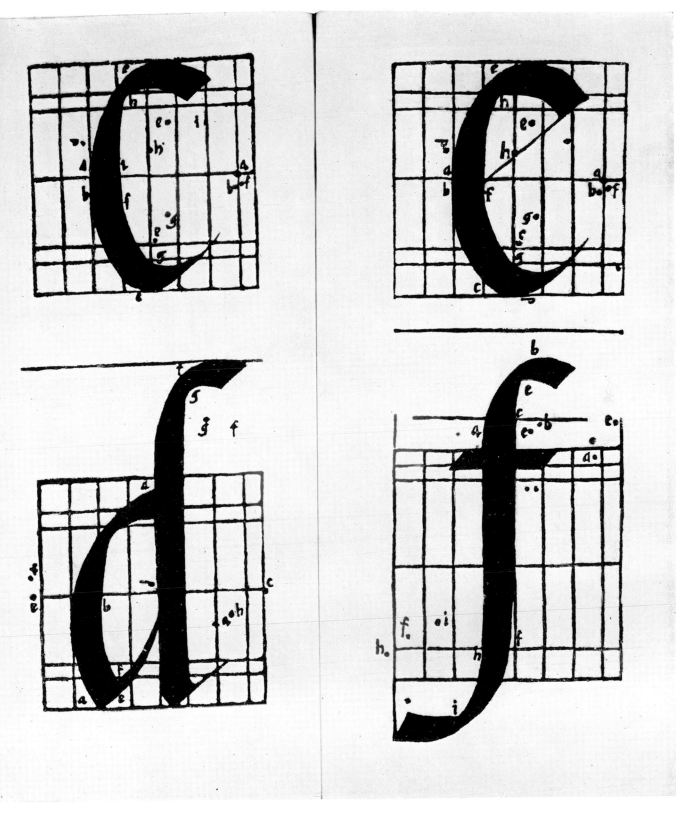

67. From *Sette Alphabeti di Varie Lettere* by Ferdinando Ruano. 1554

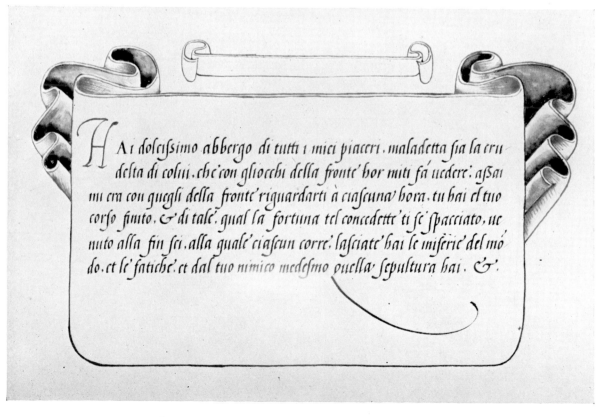

L Essere quando lo uoler è tanto
Fuor di natura, di misura torna .
Poi non sadorna di riposo mai .
Moue cangiando color, risò in piáto,
Et la figura cou paura storna ,
Poco soggiorna. Anchor di lui uedrai
Chingente di ualor lo piu si troua .

La noua qualita moue sospiri .
Et vuol chuom miri non fermato loco ,
Destandosi ira, la qual manda foco .
Imaginar nol puote huom che nol proua ,
Ne moua gia però che lui si tiri .
Et non si giri per trouarui gioco .
Ne certamente oran saper · ne poco .

68a. From a specimen book written by G. B. Palatino

H Ai dolcissimo abbergo di tutti i miei piaceri, maladetta sia la cru
delta di colui, che con gliocchi della fronte' hor miti fá uedere: assai
mi era con quegli della fronte' riguardarti à ciascuna' hora, tu hai el tuo
corso finito, & di tale, qual la fortuna tel concedette' ti se spacciato, ue
nuto alla fin sei, alla quale' ciascun corre, lasciate' hai le miserie' del mó
do, et le' fatiche, et dal tuo nimico medesmo quella' sepultura hai. &'.

68b. From a specimen book written by G. B. Palatino

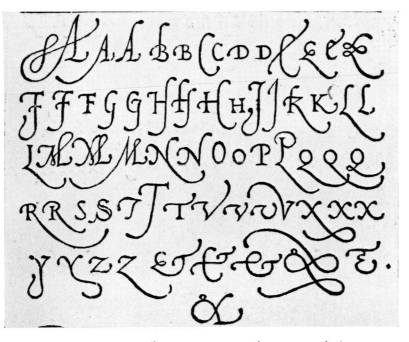

69a. From a specimen book written by G. B. Palatino

69b. From *Libro nuovo d'imparare a scrivere* by G. B. Palatino. 1540

Cancellaresca Formata.

Hor quali adunqʒ a tanti tui meriti
Potransi lode dar pari? Qual lauro
O mirto circondar à tuoi
Crini sacri di corona degna?

A a b c d e f g h i k l m n o p q
r s t u x y z.

Palatinus Romæ Scribebat
Anno Domini .
M DXXXX

Come con la esperientia della penna, potrete
uedere, seguendo il modo mio
sopradetto.

Il terzo saria appresso di loro chiama-
to Proportione quadrupla del Tra
uerso, per esser la sua
quarta parte,

Da Noi si dirà Taglio, per che
si tira co'l Taglio de la
penna,
in questa forma //

Testa — Trauerso // Taglio //

E per che alcuni potrebbono oppo=
nere, che queste Propor=
tioni et misure

70a, b. From *Libro nuovo d'imparare a scrivere* by G. B. Palatino. 1540

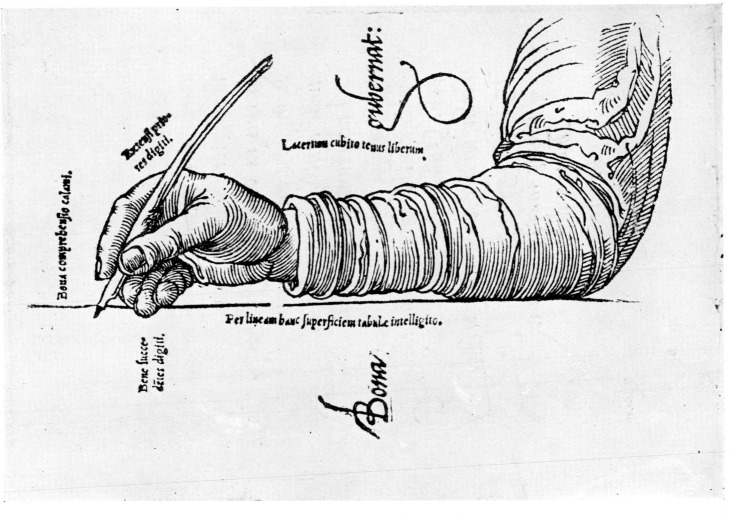

71. From *Literarum Latinarum . . . Ratio* by Gerard Mercator. 1540

72. From *Literarum Latinarum . . . Ratio* by Gerard Mercator. 1540

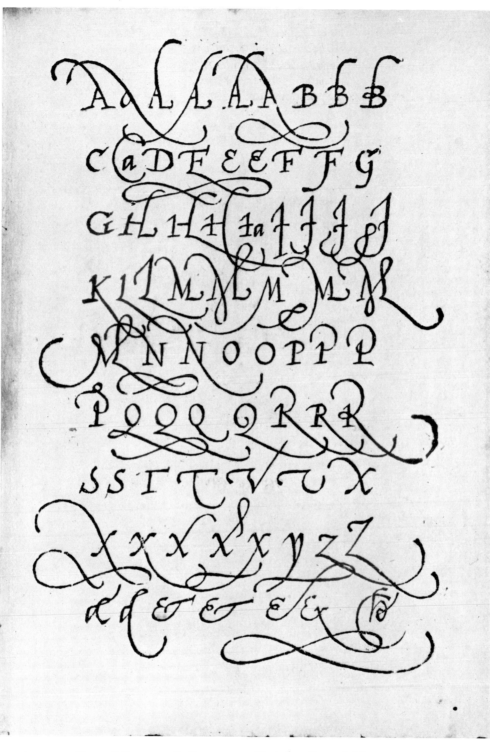

73. From *Literarum Latinarum . . . Ratio* by Gerard Mercator. 1540

VNE ESCRIPTVRE FRÃ-
coyse, laquelle on ⟶ se en ⟶ Chancellerie.

duisez que nul ne vous surpresme par Philosophie e vaine deception, selon la traditis
on des hommes, selon les institutions du monde, e non point selon Christ. Car en luy
toute plenité de divinité gist corporellement: e testes complectz en luy, qui est le
chef de toute Principaute e Puissance. Par lequel aussi estes circoncis de Circoncision faicte sans main, par le despouillement du corps des pecher, qui sont de la
chair, a savoir par la Circoncision de Christ, estans en ensevelis avec luy par le

A a b c d e f g h i k l m n o p q r ſ ſſ t u x y z c.
X. ardegg I bllk. I ſſſſſſ I ſſſſſſ ſ smntrn xyz ſ ßßß.

74. From *Thesaurium Artis Scriptoriae* by Caspar Neff. 1549

75. From a specimen book written by Vespasiano Amphiareo. 1548

g r s s

VESPASIANO · AMPHYARE
⁊ ꝼ ꞇ u MINORITANO ·

x y ꝝ 8 ℥

Grandissimo diletto gustano le humane menti benignissimo lettore nella dolce rime=
branza delli santi precetti de antichi Philosophi, et delli predarissimi fatti de inclyt, et
fortissimi Imperatori, Onde il gran stupore di natura et priape di Peripatetij, in=
segnaua ad Aless. Maced. uolgare e riuolgere gli annali della antichita da quasi se=
pre hauería trouato materia di pascer l'intelletio, e ruscare illustri. Que beneficio
in noi deriua p la sola mercede delli sacrati angelli dello antico Pallamede siglii a
mal grado del tempo ne liberano dalla obliuione di cose tanto degne et excellenti.

Al suo Giouan Battista Ciardi. A a b c d e f ff g h i ij k l m n o p

76. From *Opera nella quale si insegna a scrivere* by Vespasiano Amphiareo. 1554

77. From *Opera nella quale si insegna a scrivere* by Vespasiano Amphiareo. 1554

No teniendo cosa cierta del
mundo ni de sus cosas hazemos ca
sas costosas estando el huer
co a la puerta. Se
guimos a sathanas y a ti buen dios
no tememos de contino
te ofendemos con
los bienes que nos das.

A a b c d e f g h i k l m n o p q r
ss t v u x y z ß.

Ioannes de yciar scribebat.

1550

.I.D.V.

78. From *Arte Subtilissima* by Juan de Yciar. *c.* 1550

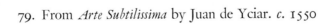

79. From *Arte Subtilissima* by Juan de Yciar. *c.* 1550

CAN CELLARESCA GR VESA

Karißima mente suplico a vra magestad tenga memoria de me mandar poner en parte donde pueda a vra magestad seruir.

A.a.b.c.d.e.f.g.h.i.k.l.m.n.o.p. g.r.ß.t.u.x.y.z.

Juan de yciar lo escriuio en çaragoça en este año de. M.D.XL.VII Λ.D.N.

80. From *Arte Subtilissima* by Juan de Yciar

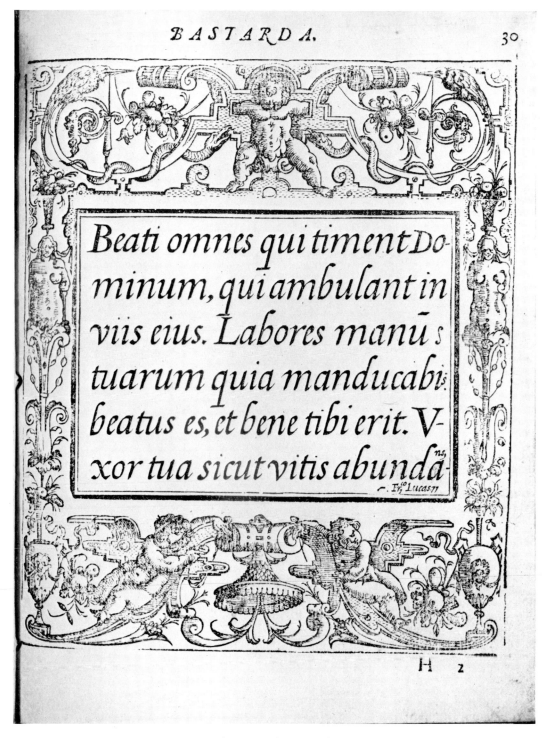

81. From *Arte de escreuir* by Francisco Lucas. 1577

Bastarda llana Mas peque
: na :
Cantate domino canticum nouum:can
tate domino omnis terra.Cantate domi
no et benedicite nomini eius: annuntia
te de die in diem salutari eius. Annun-
tiate inter gentes gloriam eius: in omni
bus populis mirabilia eius. Quoniam
magnus dominus et laudabilis nimis:
terribilis est super omnes Deos. Quoniam omnes dij gentium dæmonia
: Dominus :

Frañ Lucas Lo escreuia En

Madrid Año De M D LXX

82. From *Arte de escreuir* by Francisco Lucas

:· Bastarda grande llana :-

Obsecrote domina sancta

Maria mater Dei pietate

plenissima, summi regis fi

lia, mater gloriosissima, m̃

ter orphanorum, consola

tio desolatorum, via erran

tiuz

Fran͂ Lucas lo escreuia en

Madrid ano de M D lxx

83. From *Arte de escreuir* by Francisco Lucas

=Otro abc sin principio,
Aaa bb cc d d de eff ff f
ff g g g g g h hh b ii ſ ſ lll
m m n n oo p p p p q q r
r u ſ s ſſ ſ ſ t t t ſt t t ſt v v
v u u x x y y y z z u &
Fran.co Lucas lo eſcreuia
en Madrid año de 1570

G 2

84. From *Arte de escreuir* by Francisco Lucas

85. From the writing book of Andres Brun. 1612

coa ſb cc cod ve ſſ ccg ſ bu ſſ ſſ Ll rn

rr mm rrn co ſſ pp ccq rr ve ſſ ſs ſſt

nv uu x x w v y y zz zz z. Ett

Aaabbcc ddeeffff ff ff gg hhhiijj

ll LL mm nnoopp pqqq grrx ſſſ ss.

ſs ſſ tts tv v v uu x x y y zz z 3

bi en ha blar, es. par te. pa ra bi en. vi uir. e.
xem. plos. nun ca. ſe. to men de los ma.
los. no. tie ne per fec. to. ſu. y zio. el q̃. ga.

Sufrir coſas baxas ſin algun honeſto fun
damento, es de hombres muy viles. pocas ve
zes el liberal, es rico. El vanaglorioſo, mas
reprehenſion merece, que el mentiroſo &c

86. From *Il Perfetto Scrittore* by Gian Francesco Cresci. 1570

87. From *Lo Scrittor' Vtile et brieue Segretario* by G. A. Hercolani. 1574

88*a*. From a specimen book written by John de Beauchesne. *c.* 1570

88*b*. From *A Booke Containing Divers Sortes of Hands* by John de Beauchesne and John Baildon. 1570

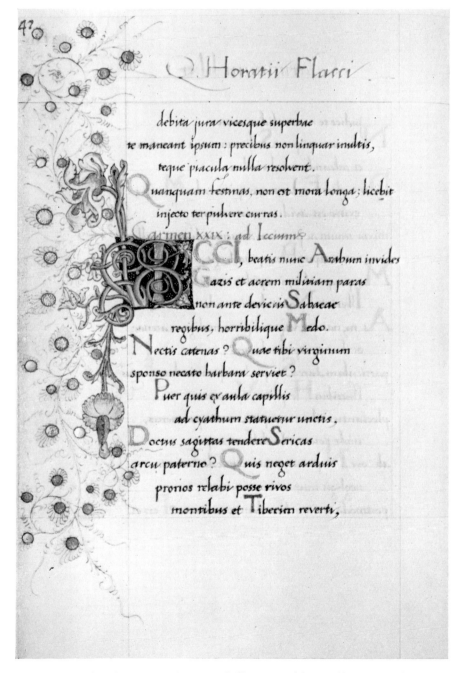

89. From *Odes of Horace* written and illuminated by William Morris. 1874

Come & sit under my stone pine that
murmurs so honey sweet as it bends to
the soft western breeze ; & lo this honey
dropping fountain, where I bring sweet
sleep, playing on my lonely reeds —

Thyrsis, the reveller, the keeper of the nymphs
sheep, Thyrsis who pipes on the reed like Pan,
having drunk at noon, sleeps under the shady
pine, & Love himself has taken the crook &
watches the flocks —

90. From *A New Handwriting for Teachers* by Mrs. M. M. Bridges. 1896

Give me my scallop shell of quiet,

My staff of faith to walk upon,

My scrip of joy, immortal diet,

My bottle of salvation,

My gown of glory, hope's true gage;

And thus I'll take my pilgrimage

91*a*. Writing by Edward Johnston. 1924

It is indeed a much more truly religious duty
to acquire a habit of deliberate, legible, and
lovely penmanship in the daily use of the
pen, than to illuminate any quantity of texts.

91*b*. From *Handwriting: Everyman's Handicraft* by Graily Hewitt.
1916

Dear Mr. Reynolds. This letter is written normally, and therefore quickly, with one of Hazell & Watson's "Esterbrook" pens. As you see I do not practise what so many preach – that all words should be written without taking off the pen. To my mind handwriting must be "natural" because it must be fast. I like to see an obviously speedy piece of script. I hate a letter which exhales the scent of some calligraphic cosmetic. Give me a true cursive, let it run as fast as one can make it and at the same time keep it sufficiently regular. If keeping the pen on an uninterrupted line helps let us by all means make it a rule to write so; but it is my experience that it is a restful and not an assistance to speed to run on or to take off at will – that will which operates automatically as the result of experience.

This is written "straight off" on unselected paper

Yours
Stanley Morison

5 April 1932

92. A letter written by Mr. Stanley Morison. 1932

Eastbourne Exeter Faversham Hove

Ipswich Lowestoft London Torquay

Aldershot Kidderminster Maldon

Newbury Nuneaton Windsor York

Croydon Gillingham Oxford Dover

Penzance Bolton Rochdale Saltash

Amazon Borneo Canada Denmark

Egypt France Gemini Holland Iraq

Jupiter Kiel Latvia Mediterranean

Niagara Ohio Popocatepetl Quebec

Russia Sweden Tasmania Uranus

Vesuvius Wales Yangtse Zambesi

93b. Dryad Writing Card by Alfred Fairbank. 1935

Some Famous Englishmen

Sir Philip Sidney, William Shakespeare,

Oliver Cromwell, John Milton,

John Bunyan, Sir Christopher Wren,

Sir Isaac Newton, Henry Purcell,

Captain Cook, Sir James Arkwright,

Lord Nelson, Duke of Wellington,

J. M. W. Turner, George Stevenson,

Michael Faraday, John Keats,

Charles Darwin, Charles Dickens.

ABCDEFGHIJKLMNOPQR
STUVWXYZ

93a. Woodside Writing Card by Alfred Fairbank. 1932

But then there's the writer who seems quite content with his ball-point "pen", who does not even think of italic. Him I should wish less to convert than to help, and in this way. I should urge him to continue with his accustomed script, but to write it with an edged pen. At once his familiar hand gains a new dimension. His old monotonous hairline letters come into a new life. The edged pen imparts to his words a flowing quality, a running sequence of alternating thicks & thins, all achieved without manual pressure. His formerly static become suddenly dynamic — not explosively but subtly & quietly, with a calm distinction as of dignified speech. The change, proceeding from the logic of the edged tool that created our Latin alphabet, may give the writer the clue to a more thorough-going reform through rediscovery of the italic hand. But even if he never takes this final step he will yet have redeemed his older script, replacing its anaemia with a timeless grace & vigor.

Yours sincerely

Paul Standard

94. Part of a letter written by Mr. Paul Standard. 1956